"IT'S NOT FAIR"

How Can We Deal with Social Challenges in Today's Culture?

Gene Matera

Printed in the United States of America

ISBN-13: 978-1-945849-52-7 paperback

CONTENTS

CHAPTER ONE

"It's Not Fair"

If a newborn could utter a few words, likely they would say, "It's not fair." From needing timely diaper changes, to proper feeding, adequate sleep, and a choice of toys, it's no wonder babies cry a lot. They cannot speak to express their needs and wants.

However, once a child learns "it's not fair," these words continue to be used throughout our lifetimes, by adolescents, teens, and adults alike. You can hear these words on the sports fields, in churches, in the work place, at home, and in schools. No one is immune. At times, these words promote social interaction and bring people together to vent, debate, and voice opinions. But in the end, saying, "It's not fair" solves and changes little, and life goes on.

Wouldn't it be great if, as children, we learned how to

cope without expecting fairness and prepared ourselves for the world's realities? "It's not fair" would be extracted from our vocabulary, and therefore our entire outlook and behavior would be different. Unfortunately, we all must endure the pain of unfairness, some of us more than others.

The difference between newborns and the rest of us is that they can't speak, don't feel hate and prejudice, and haven't been educated in societal norms. They simply live day by day, seeking life's basic needs, and when fulfilled, they are happy and content. But then, life changes.

"It's not fair" doesn't discriminate and pick favorites. The idea of fairness pertains to all cultures, races, colors, and creeds—to each one of us. Regardless of what some people may say or feel, this is the truth. Each of us has our individual experiences, stories, and evidence to prove it. And how prepared we are to cope with unfairness in life varies immensely.

Life can be more cruel than fair. It can be both cruel and unfair. And it can be just without being fair.

In June 2017, Chief Justice John Roberts delivered a commencement address at his son's ninth-grade graduation. He stated the following:

> From time to time in the years to come, I hope you will be treated unfairly, so that you will come to know the value of justice. I hope that you will suffer betrayal because that will teach you the importance of loyalty. Sorry to say, but I hope

you will be lonely from time to time so that you don't take friends for granted. I wish you bad luck, again, from time to time so that you will be conscious of the role of chance in life and understand that your success is not completely deserved and that the failure of others is not completely deserved either. And when you lose, as you will from time to time, I hope every now and then, your opponent will gloat over your failure. It is a way for you to understand the importance of sportsmanship. I hope you'll be ignored so you know the importance of listening to others, and I hope you will have just enough pain to learn compassion. Whether I wish these things or not, they're going to happen. And whether you benefit from them or not will depend upon your ability to see the message in your misfortunes.[1]

Truly inspiring and emotional comments to young students. Imagine 14-year-olds learning these lessons that many adults will never learn.

He went on to teach the students that fairness isn't about everything being equal, but about leveling the playing field so that people get what they need when they need it. When we learn the difference between equality and equity,

1 Katie Reilly, "'I Wish You Bad Luck.' Read Supreme Court Justice John Roberts' Unconventional Speech to His Son's Graduating Class," Time, July 5, 2017, http://time.com/4845150/chief-justice-john-roberts-commencement-speech-transcript/

we're on our way to understanding fairness. Unfortunately, in many instances in our society, all must receive equity regardless of their needs or merit. This is not a healthy environment for anyone.

According to an article titled "Developing a sense of fairness between ages 3 and 8," children develop egalitarianism and parochialism between the ages of 3 and 8, meaning that age is the main factor determining whether or not a child will share. The older children became, the more they were inclined to share; only 8.7% of the children in the study who were 3–4 years old shared; 45% of the children ages 7–8 shared with others.

Thus, the development to treat others with equality occurs at a young age. However, not all the children shared. Spitefulness was obvious in 14% of the children aged 7–8, which is comparable to the percentage of spiteful adults observed in other experiments.[2]

The results of the above study were observed every year, when a group of my students assisted a large community with their Easter egg hunt. There were hundreds of children, ranging from one to ten years old. The children were separated into age groups, and thousands of eggs were dropped onto a field for them to collect. Parents were asked to assist only the toddlers.

We noticed that many children shared with those who were needier, as well as those who were not. We also

2 http://www.nature.com/articles/nature07155

watched parents having fun and doing as they were asked, and others were discontented.

A child can be taught sharing and fairness at an early age. This development begins in the family and is reinforced in our schools and society.

At the age of seven, I remember parking cars at our home for the University of Wisconsin–Madison (UW–Madison, the Badgers) football games. My older sister and I had signs saying, "PARK HERE." We charged 50 cents and would fill our front yard and backyard every game. Big money in those days, especially for young kids. Heck, you could get a dozen donuts for the price of one parked car. However, an odd thing occurred in our first year as entrepreneurs: one man parked free. Our mother stated, "John would park for free." Not only did John (no friend of mine) not pay, but he also ate all our orange jelly beans, doing whatever adults at that time did while tailgating before kickoff and the short walk to Camp Randall Stadium.

I remember asking my mom why John shouldn't have to pay like all the others. Her response was "he was a family friend." End of story. Doing the quick math in my head, I realized my sister and I were losing six dollars a season. It simply was not fair!

It was the first of many times in my life that the question of fairness would surface. Of course, the later incidents would become more serious and important. The one thing I began learning early is that not everything we want or expect to be fair will be.

Coincidentally, as I was writing this, my youngest daughter called. A recent college graduate, she began her first year teaching high-school special education in central California. She is excited and feels fortunate that she was selected for the position. Her concern was that after the first three days of school, she was notified an extra class was added to her schedule. Having the normal anxiety of a first-year teacher, she exclaimed, "It's not fair." We both laughed. She knows better, but how timely.

How often do we hear people of all ages mutter these three simple words? They are serious, often angry, frustrated, and saddened.

In the Bible, Ecclesiastes 9:11 says, "Again, I observed this on earth: the race is not always won by the swiftest, the battle is not always won by the strongest; prosperity does not always belong to those who are the wisest, wealth does not always belong to those who are the most discerning, nor does success always come to those with the most knowledge—for time and chance may overcome them all." Many today struggle with this reality. They believe in infinite fairness and entitlement. They hold others responsible for their own successes or failures. Wiser people believe they deserve only what they have earned. They know they alone are responsible for their lives, and distance themselves from negative people.

Currently, many interest groups and personal causes

bury the ideals of citizenship and communities. My cause, my wants and needs, are more important than my country's.

Have we forgotten John F. Kennedy saying, "And so, my fellow Americans: ask not what your country can do for you—ask what you can do for your country"? Are his words still meaningful?

I chuckled today while reading millennials (ages 18–34) believe the government should wipe out all student loan debt. According to Independent News, "Half of all millennials would give up their right to vote in order to get rid of their student loan, according to a new survey from personal finance website Credible. Just 8.2 percent said they would choose to keep paying the debt in full and not give up anything else."

What about the students who have paid their loans in full, or the elderly who are still paying their loans off, and the parents who have student loans for their children, which far exceed students' loans. Would this debt forgiveness be fair to them?

To write off all student loans would cost the government billions of dollars, and likely result in a new tax on the rest of us who have loans. One argument, according to Student Loan Hero, is that the debt forgiveness "would go a long way towards helping millennials feel stable enough to take the next steps in their financial lives, as well as even starting businesses."[3]

3 www.fox9.com//news/42-of-americans-want-trump-to-forgive-their student-loan-debt

Although this debt elimination sounded good as a 2016 election promise, is such a plan, to forgive the debt after a certain number of years of repayment, both fair and just? Apparently not! This is just one example of millennials wanting an entitlement, masked as fairness.

It's true that college education costs today versus average wages are unfair, and students are left with huge loans without entering the workforce. Also, many argue that universities and colleges could lower tuition if institutional changes were made. Most are not made, so costs remain. However, as the pendulum swings, public college costs will decrease, and private universities also will be squeezed to lower tuitions. There is hope for our youth.

Students are fully aware what tuition costs are before they enroll in a school, although many do not understand or fail to research their loans. Some loans are better than others. Students can apply for various scholarships and grants, and work to defray costs. Again, many do, and many do not. Universities have numerous financial opportunities to assist students. It's always the student's choice.

The only differences between today and decades ago might be the work ethic and sense of entitlement. For instance, when I was in college, my father gave me one dollar for every two I earned. I must confess, I didn't like it at the start. Many of friends were playing softball and hanging out, and I was driving an Oscar Mayer meat truck. But it was a great incentive, and it worked. I had no debt and a college degree. The lesson and freedom was worth missing a few nights on the ball field and the beer fest that followed.

Few of us enjoy watching young adults incur thousands of dollars of debt. Now is a good time to grasp the moment, work together, propose ideas, and lobby politicians for student loan reform. However, this takes work, effort, and commitment. Can it be done? Yes. Will it be? That's another question.

I'm interested in the millennials because they are our biggest generation—83 million, over 25% of the US population—and they're still in the early phase of their lives. After reading up on this generation, it's safe to say some fake news regarding this group may be out there. But what is certainly true is they are ethnically more diverse than any prior generation. They are more attuned to cultural, social, political, and economic forces than their elders. They raise questions about justice and fairness, and they're often deeply concerned with the way others are treated.

Bernie Sanders was the presidential candidate of choice for most young voters. And it's true many are skeptical of capitalism; nearly half of college students say socialism is better. A Pew survey found 43% of people aged 18 to 29 have a positive opinion of socialism, compared with only 14% of people 65 and older.[4]

---

4 https://www.washintonpost.com/emilyekins/news/in-theory/ wp/20160324/millenials like socialism until they get jobs/utm term=.2ac04773

Millennials themselves will tell you they want some promises of socialism, without obligations or debt. One survey found they want free, government-funded healthcare and education, and this same group's support for socialism peaks during college. When millennials start careers making $40, 000 to $60, 000 a year, they oppose income redistribution, including raising taxes to support social programs.

There are many differences between millennials and the baby boomers, the generation that raised them. At a basic level, each generation functions differently. I doubt any of us boomers would want it any other way. Therefore, it will require both generations to have understanding, patience, and acceptance of each other. The "I told you so," "Why are you ...?" or "You need to do this or that" doesn't work with millennials.

Boomers need to remember millennials will never be just like us, and the fact is, we raised them to believe they could be and achieve everything they want. Remember saying that? Unfortunately, after getting degrees many millennials land in an economy with fewer jobs. Then, from coast to coast, one can hear the battle cry, "It's not fair."

Millennials want to work and do a good job. They quickly realize the reality of a climb up the ladder to success in any career. It's becoming evident that their definition of success may be very different than their parents.

In the end, they share many of the same values their

parents do. As they begin to have families and their children grow, don't be surprised when many tell their children, "I made mistakes, so don't ..."

Having just completed 18 years of teaching teens, I've observed many behaviors and come to many conclusions. First off, our future in the hands of these young people is not horrific, as many adults believe and fear. I was often asked, "Isn't it difficult teaching those kids?" And told, "I'm glad you are doing that—I never could." My response was always the same: "It's challenging. Most students want to be successful, and I love encouraging their potential."

It's ironic that one of the most challenging aspects of teaching isn't the student, but the parents who hold unrealistic expectations for their child and often sees worldly interactions with their child as unfair or unjust. I've never met a teacher or coach who wanted a child to fail, or intentionally went out of his or her way to ensure it.

However, teachers need to realize that this group of students and the ones preceding them are different. We can't change this, nor should we expend our energies attempting to do so. Good teachers are positive and enthusiastic. They treat all students equally and teach to their needs and potential.

This group of young adults are like all other generations: they have strengths and weaknesses. They are technology savvy, though not always patient teaching or assisting elders to use it. It was disappointing watching them attached to their phones, as if the world would stop if these devices were taken away. I often wondered what a 15-year-old could be doing, glued to their cell phone at 6:00 a.m. while walking to school, barely able to stay on the sidewalk. All kidding aside, it's dangerous. It seems that after most states have already banned cell phone use by drivers, now pedestrians may receive similar fines. I can hear it now: "It's not fair!"

Wonderful minds and bodies, take over by a phone. It's as if their purpose and passion for life is sucked out of them. Amazingly, when we took 50 or so students on an annual leadership camp into the mountains, with fun challenges and activities, and restricted cell phone use, not one student ever asked for his or her phone during the four-day camp. The students learned from this experience, that interacting with nature and one another was a marvelous part of life.

What I have learned while teaching is students through K-12 simply do not need cell phones in school to grow, learn and achieve success. Most schools throughout our nation now provide ample technology to students. The cell phone is more a distraction in the classroom than a viable learning tool and is often misused. Students often use their cell phones in lieu of paying attention and participating in group activities. When this reality occurs, and it occurs often, learning ceases. Teachers with a full class size are incapable of monitoring and policing student use, nor should they be asked to.

Therefore, it's reasonable to conclude for the health and welfare of the student and a positive learning environment, cell phones should not be authorized in schools during instruction time. This sounds drastic, but not really. It would be as natural and beneficial as weaning toddlers off pacifiers.

I believe most educators would applaud such a ruling, however, in today's environment are leery of making independent decisions based on the possible backlash from parents, unions, and students themselves. The irony is, this decision would not detract from the students learning and likely promote healthier children, children more independent, confident and capable of problem solving and doing their own thinking.

Together with their advanced technology skills, this generation is very tolerant of their peers and mankind in general. This trait always impressed me. They deplore discrimination, prejudice, and bullying. They care for one another as if in a pack, even though they don't always show it. They will generally volunteer to help their peers, school, and community, if treated with respect and a caring attitude.

Most excelled in assessments that included standardized formats (e.g., multiple choice, true or false, fill in the blank, etc.). They often demonstrated wanting to find immediate answers, complete assignments quickly, and not be bogged down in rigorous work they perceived as time-consuming, mundane, and/or useless. For many students, when asked to do critical thinking, write a paper, or present an assignment, they simply opted out and wouldn't complete the assignment.

Where they differ from previous years' groups—and I generalize—is their inability to critically think regarding issues and problems, and to communicate effectively. If it's not information they can gain from their iPad, computer, or cell phone, a panic sets in, and they shut down. In all fairness to the millennials, many have grown up in this environment of technology and social media, and they're rarely required to think for themselves and develop effective communication skills. In many cases, this has been their family life and K–12 education—their norm.

Unfortunately, this upbringing has resulted in a different kind of work ethic and mind-set: "I don't have to do it. I can pass anyway." Students are smart; they know how to get passing grades with minimal effort. This is true in the classroom and on the athletic fields. When I was young, the best time of the school day was when the final bell rang, and we went to practice with our teams. I couldn't wait—it was a blessing! However, to participate in athletics we had to perform in the classroom, whether we liked the subject or teacher, or felt the work was fair.

High-school coaches tell me that many athletes today don't want to practice, give less than 100%, and don't see the need to work hard every day. Instead of team focused, their motivations are self-focused—on what they want to do, their success, college scholarship opportunities. This makes teaching and coaching more challenging than ever before, at all age levels.

I ask myself, where have the good times gone, just playing sports for fun, without pressure from parents and schools, to excel and get scholarships?

Recently, I met a teacher who, after we began talking, was interested in my book and the topic of fairness. Without me asking, he wanted to comment. He stated, "More and more people feel they have a right to do anything they want, not considering the feelings of others." As example, he mentioned smokers subjecting others to secondhand smoke, people texting while driving and causing accidents, and people bullying and hurting others. He continued, "These individuals view fairness as 'whatever I do determines right from wrong, regardless of laws and rules.' Therefore, people must constantly be reminded of laws and rules."

He further stated, "People are often getting treated wrongly because of the actions of those committing crimes." He feels there is an increase of unsubstantiated abuse and harassment allegations, improper frisk and search, unwarranted profiling and stereotyping, false accusations, and implied guilt situations. "The rise in mistreatment," he argued, "is related to the number of similar subject criminal cases."

If he's correct, these trends are disconcerting. They have much to do with our judicial system and law enforcement programs and policies. We must always protect the accused's rights prior to evidence examination, a fair trial, and public condemnation. The latest number of sexual assault and harassment allegations is an excellent example of how individuals may take advantage of the situation for personal motives and gain.

With the current cases of mistreatment, we have an excellent opportunity to reform and change the way men and women treat each other. However, in taking this giant step forward, we must be careful not to create new injustices. All accused of all alleged crimes have rights—due process. In such a short period of time, with so many women speaking up, the daily national news and social media reports, and heightened emotions, hopefully all of this doesn't further fracture male–female relationships in schools, the workplace, and society in general. It's a natural tendency during such a high–level human rights topic to make quick assumptions and conclusions regarding a group of people. We want to rid society of sexual predators and treat all women with dignity and respect, and not, as the teacher alluded, to "wrongfully treat" the innocent. Women have a wonderful opportunity here. Let's hope we all see this through together.

And so, we wonder why young adults are growing up in the "it's not fair" world. To be honest, it's a "me" generation, with an "entitlement" mentality. It's asking for or demanding what isn't earned. It's play before work, with a YOLO (you only live once) attitude and expecting someone else to pay the tuition or bills. It's an unrealistic, unhealthy lifestyle, and the sooner it's "nipped in the bud," the better off we all are.

The good news is, this generation will eventually figure it out, though this process may result in a painful learning curve. It's a generation unlike the one many of us grew up in, a generation we don't know, like, or have tolerance for. It's a generation that will continue to question fairness, where there is lack of accountability for personal decision making, and initiative burns out when they face adversity and challenges.

Many millennials have been raised to believe that if they got a good education and were good kids, life would be easy. They're learning that isn't how life always works out. And they say, "It's not fair."

Special interest groups are a group of people or an organization seeking special advantages, such as government, political, religious, and social groups and organizations. America has its fair share of special interest groups, and the lists seems to keep growing. These groups are expanding throughout many countries, and we're beginning to see more movements throughout the world.

Many of these movements are extremely complicated, with various issues and problems, and the questions of fairness and justice are intertwined in their cultures.

Culture is such a broad term. Let's safely say that solutions to problems are difficult, with the need to include religious, political, economic, and human rights concerns.

To narrow this down, let's examine social movements in the US. Social movements involve groups of people who protest in marches, sit-ins, picketing, lobbying, and occasionally violence, and have always been part of the American system and politics, used by both the left and right. The object is to disrupt the functioning of some institution, to force it to negotiate with the group's needs and wants, and to enlist the support of others (often the media) or to provoke attacks and arrests, so martyrs are created.

For hundreds of years, social movements have promoted their goals through nonviolence. The Quakers, Mahatma Gandhi, the Dalai Lama, Nelson Mandela, and Martin Luther King Jr, come to mind. These people led nonviolent movements that were all considered successful.

According to Biography on Line, "Gandhi frequently called off strikes and nonviolent protest if he heard people were rioting or violence was involved."[5]

His goal was clear: for India to have self-government. He used a nonviolent path to lead the Indians to independence. To Gandhi, the road to the goal was equally important to the goal itself. Gandhi's quotes are inspiring; however, in today's society, they're seemingly forgotten and irrelevant.

5 https://www.biographyonline.net// politicians/indian/gandhi.html

One quote is particularly applicable today: "I object to violence because, when it appears to do good, the good is only temporary; the evil it does is permanent."[6]

Have we learned and applied our knowledge from these peaceful activists, or are they just pretty slogans and quotes in textbooks or classrooms, or repeated in churches or by motivational speakers? One worthy quote thoroughly taught and discussed can be more powerful than a book full of information.

In the 1960s, Vietnam War protests changed everything. Opposition to the Vietnam War united groups opposed to communism, imperialism, colonialism, and capitalism. The opposition to our military involvement grew, eventually turning US political opinion against the war. The press had a heyday publishing "underground papers" fueling the protest and protesters. Peaceful protest changed to riots, bombings, violence, destruction, and death itself in our own country.

In 1970, I was just entering high school, and will always remember the bombing that occurred at 3:42 a.m. on August 24, at the Army Mathematics Research Center, Sterling Hall, UW–Madison. Four men protesting the Vietnam War used a car bomb to destroy the building and nearby buildings. The bombing killed a researcher, who was a father of three, and injured three other employees. The bombing occurred two miles from my family's home. I didn't understand then, and do not today. It wasn't fair!

6 https://www.brainyquote.com//quotes/mahatma gandhi/125824

Some will say this violent movement was necessary, that the eventual US withdrawal in Vietnam wouldn't have occurred without it, and it produced a positive outcome for American society. It was a productive voice challenging our nation's political systems, our prolonged involvement and moral responsibility in world affairs, and the people's right to assemble and speak freely. The movement certainly struck the nation's conscience.

As effective as social movements are (some more than others), they can also be destructive rather than constructive. The activism in the 1960s also introduced, and to some degree legitimized, violent protest into our society. Today, violence is a common occurrence, and there seems to be no turning back.

The protesters wanted the US to withdraw from the war and to change Americans' social conscience. They wanted peace and love, not prolonged war and killing. Worthy goals and causes at the time. For the most part, the "hippies" had passion and resolve for the human race.

Certainly, US involvement in Vietnam for over a decade was tragic, with much blame to go around. The prolonged affair was destined for debate, protest, and social revolution. The "lessons learned" fill a military training pamphlet and Congressional records.

Being old enough to remember, I often reflect on many of the protest leaders, non-Americans and others mainly intent on overthrowing our government by violent means.

The followers, many yearning for attention and acceptance, needed a group to belong to. For many, it was a timeframe used to escape into a lethargic life of drugs, sex, and zombie-ism. For others, it was peaceful and passionate demonstration for love, not war. They pled for peace.

Unfortunately, our military men and women became entangled between the American people and the government. Many protestors saw the military as part of the problem rather than part of the solution. This feeling and attitude toward our service members persisted during and after the war. Many veterans were unprepared for this outcome. For many, their welcome home wasn't what it should have been.

Did our military men and women deserve this treatment? It's well known that our civilian leaders and politicians were the primary decision makers in the Vietnam War. Our field commanders had little input and were rarely consulted until much later in the war. This was a major mistake and future lesson. Nevertheless, our service men and women suffered because of it.

Our men and women fought valiantly, even though politically constrained in Vietnam, because it was their duty. They swore an oath to serve and defend all Americans, and they swore to obey all orders of those appointed over them. This is the way they were trained—to follow the chain of command and to obey all legal orders.

Those serving in Vietnam did this, with some exceptions,

to the best of their abilities.

Our men and women fought with honor, courage, and commitment, until hope was lost. In Vietnam, American involvement became mismanaged, decision making was flawed at the highest levels, military authority was undermined, and support from home dwindled. Understandably, troop morale steadily declined. To the men and women in uniform, "It wasn't fair."

The Vietnam War divided America as much as any conflict, including the Civil War. Our government lacked leadership and character and therefore lost its citizenry support.

I always told stories to my students with an intended purpose and goal. Many involved a part of the curriculum, leadership, character, morality, and being responsible citizens. I made my points, without getting too deep, preaching, or providing my opinion, and with some humor, if possible. My humor wasn't always theirs and vice versa, but that's a different subject!

One topic I discussed yearly with all my students was that along with being productive and caring citizens, they needed to like themselves, love themselves, and be their own best friend. Only then would they be capable of loving others.

They should be comfortable with looking at themselves in a mirror and seeing inner beauty, honesty, and compassion. That it's all right to talk to oneself, literally, and I challenged them to try it. Have an inner round-table discussion occasionally with me, myself, and I, and you'll find inner peace and freedom, I would tell them, for the only thing we fully control is our own minds.

Many of my students laughed at the absurdity of locking oneself up in the bathroom with the family dog and self-reflecting in a mirror. I knew this wasn't a teen thing; however, some of my students did it. And once comfortable with who they were, I challenged them over a few weeks to form personal values and goals in their lives. These were hard, challenging lessons, but most took it seriously and enjoyed it.

My students began to realize they have little or no control of the outside world, but can make their inside world an honorable, strong, and safe place to be. Having established this inner peace, they would be better able to confront and overcome the question of fairness in their lives. Me, myself and I. I always remember the quote, "To thine own self be true."[7]

And the Serenity Prayer, written by Reinhold Niebuhr, says it much better than I ever could: "God, give us grace to accept with serenity the things that cannot be changed, Courage to change the things which should be changed, and the Wisdom to distinguish one from the other."[8]

Despite all the good advice people provide and receive,

7 http:/enotes.com//internet/enotes/Shakespeare quotes/hamlet act 1, scene 3, 78-82
8 http://skdesigns.com/internet/articles/prose/niebuhr/serenity_prayer/

the problem is that good advice is often extraordinarily difficult to follow. I believe it takes repetition and self-examination. If one wants to be truthful every day, that person must make a concerted effort and practice honesty, and reflect on and examine their daily behavior. All negative behaviors, rationalization, projection, and self-pity, must be discarded. Make the goal zero tolerance for poor behavior and excuses.

Many activists haven't learned that to achieve their goals, they must have leaders with character and virtue. If we want to be heard, we must listen. If we want to be heard, we must act in a nonviolent, respectful way. This doesn't mean that a group must be subservient, agree, or be coerced to stop its cause. What it does mean is that if the cause is important enough to a group, that it will be civil, truthful, and respectful.

The priority should always be achieving the goal, not the actions of a few who may deviate because of personal agendas. Without leadership, followers drift, the group loses credibility and audience, and becomes nothing more than a weathered and tattered sail in a storm, as many groups did in the 1960s.

According to Greg Satell of the *Harvard Business Review*, for a movement to truly make an impact, it must have five steps. First, clearly define the change and goal(s) desired. Gandhi wanted independence from the British; the civil rights movement wanted specific legislation. The color revolutions wanted a leadership change.[9]

Also, successful movements identify and recruit institutional groups, such as the police, media, education system, or government agencies. Without this support, little is likely to change. Another step applicable today is to attract people, not overpower them. Basically, getting along with others is more productive, for anger alone is a destructive force.

Gandhi wrote, "We win justice quickest by rendering justice to the other party or group." Therefore, blocking streets, throwing rocks, and looting stores turns off potential allies and justice and the cause is lost. If we know this, why have violent protests become common occurrences?

At the July 2017 G-20 Summit in Germany, world leaders were endangered by protestors who blocked roads and became violent, ignited by a small bloc of anarchists who saw the summit as the perfect platform for their rejection of capitalism and order. These weren't the specific causes or perceived injustice of the 100,000 or so peaceful demonstrators who marched during the summit. The protestors' credibility and voice was lost, as they met swift police resistance.

Maybe one of the most intolerable and disappointing realities today is individuals or groups who emotionally cry, "It's not fair," but challenge justice and fairness with apathy

9 https://hbr.org//Satell & Popovic/201701/how protests become successful social movements

or hypocrisy. Many activists have little knowledge of simple American civics, know little about our political system, or in some cases, even about the issues they adamantly and proudly advocate for. Just to protest—saying, "We want this," and "It's not fair"—doesn't cut it. Students are good examples of this type of behavior.

Todd Gitlin, a Columbia University professor, said the following about college students this way, "Most students at most times are apathetic in that whatever they think or think they think, they have other priorities besides stepping up and doing political work."[10]

To be fair, in this respect today's students are like most of us navigating our way, inexperienced in the real world and to some degree idealistic. Real activism, however, demands more than this.

According to "How We Killed Expertise," a *POLITICO* magazine article, "most Americans think a quarter of the U.S. federal budget is devoted to foreign aid, when more than 70 percent cannot name all three branches of government—and nearly a third can't name even one—the basic structures of American democracy cannot survive."[11]

Most of us realize that if you poll only millennials on basic civics and American history, it gets much worse than this—almost to a point that you don't know whether to laugh or cry.

10 http://www.thedartmouth.com/article/2016/02/how-effective-is-social-media-activism/
11 https://www.politico.com/magazine/nichols/story/05092017/how we killed expertise -215531

The article continues,

> The Founding Fathers believed that civic virtue was built on education and knowledge. In a republic, citizens need not be experts, but they must learn enough to cast an informed vote. Or, in the words of James Madison: 'A people who mean to be their own Governors must arm themselves with the power which knowledge gives.' If Americans do not rediscover this foundational truth about their own system of government, they not only court disasters from pandemics to wars; they risk ceding their government either to the corruption of a mindless mob—or, in the wake of a disaster, to a new class of technocrats who will never again risk asking for their vote.

Recently in my class, we taught 15 and 16-year-olds the US Constitution and Declaration of Independence. Amazingly, few had ever seen these documents and had no idea how they came to be, who was involved, the timeframe in which they occurred, and their significance to our country.

We started from the beginning. Each student had their own pocket-size pamphlet, which they thought was cool and brought to class daily. We read every word together, and they absorbed the material as if they realized it was important. They returned each day having studied the material and were prepared to discuss it. I wonder if our history and civics is no longer important enough to teach or prioritize in our schools. Have these subjects been replaced in the modern, technological world?

Many today are involved in activism using social media. Is it effective? I'd say yes to some degree, but the potential of social media alone is no more than 10% of the pie. It can be a way to communicate, organize, and raise awareness. It may challenge people to think about certain issues and opinions they otherwise might not have known or considered. And it's far-reaching, able to pull people together for an action or event. However, there are limitations on the benefits of social media to instill justice and fairness.

First, the use of social media is not a movement. People won't create change and influence justice merely through social media. Facebook and Twitter entries galore cannot replace personal involvement.[12] Most of us know people who are compelled to use social media to inform and "teach" the rest of us. This form of communication is rarely productive and more so, self-serving. What do you suppose the number of social media "activists" is versus those who have a physical role in their cause?

Understandably, most social media users aren't activists. They type for a few minutes a day, provide their opinions, refer to the opposition, and then are off to their daily routines. It's the easy way. Do they really believe

---

12 *Shonda Rhimes quotations in The Dartmouth article: http://www.
thedartmouth.com/article/2016/02/how-effective-is-social-media-
activism/*

others care or are interested? Only a few people or groups keep an open dialogue over a given time, and for these few, it's normally one sided, jaded, and emotional. You can anticipate the tone and words: self-satisfying, probably; productive to society, doubtful.

So get off your electronics, and get moving. Not many young adults today enjoy politics. They are skeptical of the political system and have a lack of trust and hope in national affairs. Some of this feeling and belief is fair, and some not. All politicians are not evil and self-serving, democracy is not crumbling, and our judicial system is not completely corrupted and discriminatory. There are a tremendous number of honest, hardworking, and serving government employees.

We're not a perfect system and never have been. It's time to speak up, listen, learn, and get active in life, or be contently apathetic, unknowledgeable, and disenchanted. We all have a choice.

Pendulum changes occur in many aspects of life. Politics is no different. I would argue that for our youth, what better time than now to serve in government office and influence change?

To quit, do nothing, and/or play "Monday morning quarterback" is the easy way out. If people make government service a career step, have character, and have prepared themselves morally with the principles of equity and justice, they'll be successful and well served.

Randolph Byrd, in his short poem "Fairness," is concise:[13]

Because we are so human,

It is important to realize,

that is more important to try to be fair,

than always reaching that lofty goal.

After all,

"Ye without sin, cast the first stone."

Hopefully, we conclude "it's not fair" applies to all humans. We all have experienced unfairness and have coped with it in our own ways. Unfairness can be very painful, and potentially destructive, if we allow it to be.

The ideal, "fair" world doesn't exist. What can exist is our acceptance of this truth and the way we live our lives preparing for and coping with reality. No one can tell another how to do this; we each must find our own way. A good remembrance and daily repetition is this: Know yourself, be true to yourself and others, and go forward. Time is a great healer if we let it be one. After all, what choice do we have?

---

13 https://www.poetrysoup.com//Randolph Byrd/poem/fairness 781445/2016

CHAPTER TWO

Am I Living in a Just World?

"Justice is the legal or philosophical theory by which fairness is administered. The concept of justice differs in every culture ... as cultures are dependent upon shared history, politics, mythology and/or religion" (Wikipedia)[14]. Justice in America involves the citizens' agreement regarding the ethics and values we want to live by. Our country's justice formulates and drives fairness. Justice is fairness's older sister; they are bonded. In theory, a culture has both or neither.

Justice in America began in Congress on July 4, 1776, with the Declaration of Independence, and the assertion "that all men are created equal, that they are endowed by their Creator with certain unalienable Rights, that among these are Life, Liberty, and the pursuit of Happiness."

14 *https://en.wikipedia.org/wiki/justice*

American justice, therefore, ensures individuals equality of opportunity and what they deserve, merit, or are entitled to. Our own laws, principles, religions, and politics often conflict with true justice.

In 1918, there was a nationwide contest for writing a national creed, which was to summarize the American political faith, founded upon things fundamental in American history and tradition. At the time, patriotism was low. The US had been participating in World War I for a little over a year.

Over three thousand entries were received, and William Tyler Page's "The American's Creed" was declared the winner. Referring to the creed, Page wrote, "It is the summary of the fundamental principles of American political faith, as set forth in its greatest documents, its worthiest traditions, and by its greatest leaders."[15] His wording of the creed used passages and phrases from the Declaration of Independence, the Preamble to the Constitution, and Lincoln's Gettysburg Address: "I believe in the United States of America as a government of the people by the people, for the people, whose just powers are derived from the consent of the governed, a democracy in a republic, a sovereign Nation of many sovereign States; a perfect Union, one and inseparable; established upon those principles of freedom, equality, justice, and humanity for which American patriots sacrificed their lives and fortunes.

15 www.fighting patriot.com//story/%20%behind%20the%20american%20 creed.html

"I therefore believe it is my duty to my Country to love it, to support its Constitution, to obey its laws, to respect its flag, and to defend it against all enemies."[16]

The American's Creed is a wonderful document to teach. Students like it—it's simple, clear, and concise. They remember it, and maybe refer to it. Isn't this what we want for our youth, when justice fails them and fairness is lost in darkness?

A just society accompanied with fairness is what each American expects; it's part of our DNA. When this system fails us, and it does, it's no wonder we observe negative behavior. Justice is like fairness: both are ideals the world fails to live up to, either deliberately or not. It's an inevitable truth, and because we are human, one that will never change.

We're all better off understanding this reality and accepting it. We don't have to like it, and certainly shouldn't be submissive and dormant. We need to continue working together and communicating to maintain our basic morals, values, and principles. Without these basic building blocks, little justice and fairness can occur.

Justice, or the lack of it, is eternally everywhere, and binds each of us. We should never be shortsighted and assume justice only applies in the realm of our local, state, and federal government—i.e., Congress, judicial systems, and the president. However, a political system

---

16 *www.usflag.org//american.creed.htm*

in any country is necessary to create, maintain, supervise, and continuously sculpt justice. Therefore, politics in any culture is important to the development and sustainment of justice.

Any team, organization, or group of people, no matter how big or small, will take on the personality, mood, and morale of its leadership. Countries are no different. There are numerous examples past and present, in our country and others, validate leadership's importance. If leadership is ineffective, stumbles, or even fails, the followers lose confidence, become resistant, and speak out. Morale often declines, and conflict eventually occurs. Justice is negatively affected.

What kind of justice did or do the people have under Hitler, Stalin, Pol Pot, Augusto Pinochet, Saddam Hussein, Idi Amin, Kim Jong-il, Francisco Franco, and recently, Bashar al-Assad and Kim Jong-un? These ruthless dictators put their self-serving wants and needs ahead of justice for their people. Stalin himself said, "Lenin founded our state, and we've screwed it up."[17] Each of these leaders failed to create a just environment, where people were treated equitably and at the very least humanely. And of course, they received or receive little from their people in return.

We have accomplished wonderful successes throughout our nation's young history, but even so, we find ways to retreat and hunker down in our trenches and miss grand

17 www.historyinan hour.com//20110701/stalinsbreakdown/posted from the Sixth Man by Rupert Colley

opportunities. We must continue to be steadfast and patient, recognizing that change is constructive and necessary and involves conflict, hard work, and time. It is always time for action and results; words alone are powerless.

According to CNN, a report produced by the International Labor Organization (ILO) states, "More than 40 million people worldwide were estimated to be victims of slavery in 2016—and one in four of those were children." The report estimates that in 2015, "25 million people were in forced labor—made to work under threat or coercion— and 15 million people were in forced marriage." Regarding child labor, the report states, "90 percent of all children in child labor are in the Africa and the Asia and the Pacific regions."[18]

These numbers are astounding, as more research is being conducted to determine the magnitude of these injustices and human rights violations.

As the world progresses in the treatment of human life, we have plenty of work and challenges ahead. Global leaders established worldwide goals to be achieved by 2030, to end forced labor, modern slavery, and human trafficking, as well as child labor in all its forms. Can the US lead in enacting this change?

So, are you living in a just world? No one can answer that question but you. It's your perception of the world you live in. Your answer should be based on an educated

18 http://cnn.com//internet/newsreport/mark tutton/40 million slaves in the world, finds new report//09/20/2017

understanding of America's past, present, and future. An honest answer can only be made if you consider fairness and justice for all, over any sole issue/cause.

There are many success stories in our history, some with ongoing progress. Women's rights are a proud example of a successful movement. Women have increased their rights, nonviolently, from an initial position of powerless, and against intense opposition. They have accomplished much through meetings, lobbying, rallies, petitions, public speaking, and nonviolent resistance.

This success has taken time, hard work, and diligence. They have persevered not only for their own sake, but also to be productive contributors to humankind. The batons have been passed over the decades, gracefully, with leadership, optimism, and hope. Women have succeeded; however, their work isn't done. A quote attributed to Margaret Mead says, "Never doubt that a small group of thoughtful, committed citizens can change the world; indeed, it's the only thing that ever has."

Women, like other groups, have been discriminated against. Elizabeth Cady Stanton, using the Declaration of Independence as a framework for writing what she titled a "Declaration of Sentiments" wrote, "the history of mankind is a history of repeated injuries and usurpations on the part of man toward woman, having in direct object the establishment of an absolute tyranny over her."[19]

Today, it's hard to imagine that even as late as the mid–1800s women had few rights. They couldn't vote until 1920, and it wasn't until the 1960s when our politicians began serious conversations regarding women in the workplace. According to the National Women's History Project, "With the inclusion of Title IX in the Education Codes of 1972, equal access to higher education and to professional schools became the law. The number of women doctors, lawyers, engineers, architects, and other professionals has doubled and doubled again as quotas actually limiting women's enrollment in graduate school were outlawed."[20]

Athletics has also changed dramatically with Title IX. Girls' and women's participation in athletics has soared. According to Women's Sports Foundation, "Before Title IX, one in 27 girls played sports. Today that number is two in five." The National Women's History Project states, "Women are now active in sports at all levels, including professional athletics and our US Olympic teams."[21]

There are many other issues where women have prevailed in achieving justice, personal freedoms and expanded opportunities. As a father of three wonderful daughters, I'm grateful that they each can develop their

19 www.digitalhistory.uh.edu//disp.textbook.cfm smtid=3+psid=382/ Elizabeth Cady Stanton "Address Delivered at Seneca Falls" CR 2016 Digital History
20 www.nwhp.org//resources/womensrights movement/history of the womens' rights movement/ Eisenberg & Ruthsdotter/National Womens' History Project,1998
21 https://womenssportsfoundation.org//internet/articles/maegan olmstead/Title IX and the Rise of Female Athletes in America/09/02/2016

unique skills and talents and pursue their dreams.

Do they believe they live in a just world? I don't know; it's their perception. But one thing is clear: many women and men have paved a new trail for them.

What I do know about my daughters is that they believe strongly in women's rights; however, they wouldn't want to be labeled "feminists." My guess is that they don't want to be labeled. They favor all qualified women, in any occupation, receiving equal opportunity and treatment. However, if unqualified, then women should receive no special treatment. In other words, no arbitrary selection of a woman to a position she's unqualified for or doesn't have the potential to assume because "it's time," "we need a ...," or "females are superior to males," and so forth. The same applies to unqualified males.

Women today simply don't need the extremism and buzzwords to be successful; they're doing quite well without them. Many, in fact, resent this dangerous agenda. Most women have the richness of their own knowledge and experiences, coupled with self-esteem, to move forward in life. They don't need society labeling them.

Emotionally healthy women don't have adversarial attitudes, inferiority complexes, or extremism in their lives. This lobbying and negativity is burdensome and only a distraction. They would much prefer to use their strengths and energy pursuing success and happiness. These women are less vocal, moving forward with action.

As important as women are to our society and the work force, let's not forget the women who continue to make choices, sometimes difficult ones, to stay home with their children. They often are marginalized, by women themselves.

My mother, intelligent and extremely gifted, stayed home and raised four of us, never questioning her decision. Her work, strength, and love had a direct impact on our lives. Her daily work and responsibility was as, if not more, challenging as any position in the work force. After all of us left home, she received a medical degree and went to work.

My daughters will always want to be considered based on their talents, ability, and merit. They expect to be treated with equality, respect, and dignity in the workplace. They know women's history and suffering, and see the brightness and hope in the future. I imagine they feel fortunate living in today's society, and don't take it for granted.

There is more work to be done regarding justice for women. Men and women, together, will continue to resolve these issues peacefully. Alice Paul, who first wrote out the Equal Rights Amendment in 1923, said, "I always feel the movement is a sort of mosaic. Each of us puts in one little stone, and then you get a great mosaic at the end."[22]

The women's movement has been tremendously successful, an example of where justice prevailed in America, though the journey has been long, painful, and hard fought.

22 https://www.goodreads.com//quotes/paul/44995 I always feel the movement is a sort of mosaic

Why do we not use this movement's story, history, and success as the benchmark for all social movements?

An example today of a missed opportunity is developing an equitable and fair health plan for all Americans—the young, elderly, poor, chronically ill, mentally ill, etc. It's baffling that the issue of ensuring people's healthcare has become so difficult to agree upon. Why?

The Affordable Care Act (ACA), (sometimes referred to as Obamacare) the comprehensive healthcare reform law, was signed by President Obama in March 23, 2010. Just two days earlier, all Republicans voted against it. Congressional members argued that the law had been so constantly changed and was so cumbersome that few members from both parties had the opportunity to read and study it, and for those who had, many didn't understand it.

According to David Bernstein, in his article "Let's Recall Why the Affordable Care Act Is So Messed Up," says, "The Democratic leadership, fearful that momentum for Obamacare was fading as it continued to poll poorly, decided to rush a bill through the Senate before Christmas 2009." It's worth pausing a moment to remember how the law was passed, and why "various inconsistencies, ambiguities, internal contradictions, and other problems [that] were not just predictable but inevitable."[23]

Evidently, only experts could interpret the law. Why

23 *https://www.washingtonpost.com//news/volokhconspiracy/bernstein/ up/2015/06/25 /let's recall why the Affordable Care Act is so messed Up/ utm term = .930015f467a0*

rush any law—particularly one of this magnitude—impacting the health and welfare of so many, without all lawmakers (absent input from their constituents) being able to ascertain whether it's a "good" law or not? Was it more important to the administration to pass a major law even while realizing the legislation wasn't thorough and needed time for more close examination?

Fast forward to today. The Republicans and the president are attempting to repeal and replace Obamacare. How hard they are trying. During the 2016 election, they made a campaign pledge to Americans to do so. Not the first time politicians have made promises they are unable or unwilling to fulfill.

Their second effort to repeal Obamacare was defeated in the Senate. The decision-making process hasn't been inclusive. Small groups of Republicans working together behind closed doors seemingly believed they needed little input, opinion, or expertise but their own. Their thinking, resistance to collaboration, and stubbornness to pass quick legislation was doomed from the beginning. Clearly, both parties working together would have been more productive.

Frustrating, though Americans are getting used to this. It's been going on for years. Senator John McCain, who voted against repealing ACA, responded, "I've stated time and time again that one of the major failures of Obamacare was that it was rammed through Congress by Democrats on a strict-party line basis without a single Republican vote.

We must now return to the correct way of legislating and send the bill back to committee, hold hearings, receive input from both sides of [the] aisle, heed the recommendations of [the] nation's governors, and produce a bill that finally delivers affordable health care for the American people."[24]

We haven't done so. Justice, hardly! Seven years later, and we are no closer to providing affordable health care to all Americans.

This trend continued in December 2017, when the Senate passed Republicans' tax legislation with no Democratic support. The legislation, 479 pages long, was rushed overnight on December 2, giving both the public and legislators themselves little or no time to review it. "Not a single member of this chamber has read the bill," Senate Minority Leader Chuck Schumer said. "It would be impossible."[25]

Every Democratic senator voted against the bill. Senator Jon Tester from Montana commented that the bill was "Washington, D.C., at its worst,"[26] as he held up a ream of paper a few inches thick. Much of the document had handwritten changes in the margins. The tax plan is full of questions, loopholes, and other potential problems that could plague lawmakers long after the legislation becomes law. Also concerning is how Americans can comply with

24 https://www.mccain.senate.gov/public/index.cfm/2017/7/statement by Senator McCain on voting no on skinny repeal/
25 https://www.cbsnews.com/news/democrats outraged over senate gops last minute tax bill reveal/
26 https://www.nytimes.com//internet/articles/Tankersley & Rappeport/A Hasty, Hand-Scribbled Tax Bill Sets Off on Outcry//12012017

this law if it's enacted by January 1. "Montanans deserve so much better," Sen Tester tweeted.

Have our politicians learned anything from the ACA's drawing up and implementation? Apparently not.

How do Americans view our executive, legislative, and judicial systems? If you're in tune, you know most Americans would answer, "Not well!" We view government officials fighting each other, acting in secrecy, and making decisions based on party affiliation alone, and not necessarily for the betterment of the people. American leadership is lacking in all three government branches, and has been for many years. Until this reality changes, our country is stuck in neutral while important social issues linger.

So, when we view justice in one area of life, we often don't view it in another. Red and blue America. Congress, the president and judicial system. Law enforcement and the people. Minorities and special interest. Our educational system, students' and parents' needs. Environmental concerns and healthcare. An immigration program and our laws. An equitable and streamlined (simpler) tax system. All these issues center around justice and should be first approached with consideration of the equality, welfare, and security of all people.

Justice is either grace and beauty or evil and ugliness. There are literally thousands of books, articles, classes, writings, and lectures on justice in America. Many take opposing views, some declare "little justice" based on isolated incidents/actions, and others feel justice occurs, but too often doesn't. And some feel that with our everyday faults and stumbles, we're just society. Justice is an individual perception, one we must constantly monitor and never ignore.

As Justice Lewis Powell said, "Equal justice under law is not a merely a caption on the facade of the Supreme Court building; it is perhaps the most inspiring ideal of our society. It is one of the ends for which our entire legal system exists. It is fundamental that justice should be the same, in substance and availability, without regard to economic status."[27] He's right, but is this consistently occurring?

Years ago, a 17-year-old kid was playing with his American Legion baseball team in a twi-night doubleheader far from his hometown. In the second game, he pitched 16 innings and lost 1-0. The game ended late, and the boys, accompanied by their coach, went to their dormitory on a women's college campus.

Shortly after, the pitcher and a few teammates snuck out. Sometime later, the police arrived and arrested all the players. They were all given the same citations—drinking under age, breaking and entering, and causing minor damage. All the players except for the pitcher were apprehended inside a women's dormitory. The pitcher was found sleeping at the doorstep.

As it turns out, the pitcher never entered the building,

27 www.texasatj.org/what access justice Justice Lewis Powell, Jr

and another ballplayer broke the door. Even so, they all received the same punishment. It was equitable treatment, but was it just and fair?

There are many stories, great and small, of injustice and unfair treatment. Law enforcement in one city is different than another, states criminal laws are often different, and judge's interpretation of the law and sentencing practices vary.

For justice to prevail in any society, all judiciary matters must be separated from the political system. The checks and balances in a democracy must remain intact for good reason.

President Lincoln wasn't oblivious to fairness and justice. How could he be, having been born poor? He envisioned the American government as an institution providing citizens opportunities, and not a system mandating "fairness." Under a government of laws, Lincoln felt all men should have the freedom to acquire property of their own free will. That won't guarantee the same results for everyone. In the case of those who didn't get wealthy, the solution wasn't to spread the wealth by interposing the hand of power: "Let not him who is houseless pull down the house of another, but let him laborwork diligently and build one for himself."[28]

Lincoln was concerned that even government could become too powerful, especially if it took on the appearance of dispensing fairness and social reform. He stated, "The

28 https://www.firstthings.com/webexclusives/Guelzo/2010/02/Lincoln and justice for all/2.15.10

legitimate object of government, is to do for a community of people, whatever they need to have done, but cannot do, at all, or cannot, so well do, for themselves. That government shouldn't reach toward the involvement in and settlement of inequities in property, talent, wealth, industriousness, or self-esteem, and if it did, that would bring down both fairness and law. The proposition that each man should do precisely as he pleases with all which is exclusively his own lies at the foundation of the sense of justice there is in me. I extend the principles to communities of men as well as to individuals."[29]

President Lincoln's words remind us that the real dangers of fairness and justice in our society aren't the weakness of the people and their abilities, but the possibilities of an overly powerful government. We have been trending in this direction over the past few decades.

Equality before the law is a wonderful principle. When written into our Constitution, it was undeniably and clearly unlike all others and practiced nowhere else in the world. In the recent past, much has occurred to draw us away from this founding principle.

We find hundreds of executive orders signed over the past decade, due to our nation's division and Congress's inability to work together. A working democracy shouldn't have this issue.

We find judges at all levels determining cases based

29 https://www.firstthings.com/webexclusives/Guelzo/2010/02/Lincoln and justice for all/2.15.10

on their own political views and inconsistent with the Constitution and judicial precedent. When exposed, they be should be relieved from the bench.

We find career politicians who accept campaign cash from corporate interests, while concurrently campaigning against this practice. If exposed, they shouldn't be reelected.

We find telecoms and government agencies illegally wiretapping and spying on selected groups and citizens. Rather than be granted immunity, the perpetrators should be prosecuted.

We find large institutions committing financial fraud. If guilty, these institutions should be penalized, fined, or cease to exist.

We find politicians, celebrities, professional athletes, business leaders, and other prominent figures committing crimes daily, and often their cases are dismissed.

We find a law enforcement system that occasionally targets certain groups of people or individuals without probable cause. Enforcement and treatment isn't always equitable.

Law enforcement needs to ensure they hold their own accountable—zero tolerance.

My sister, a writer as well, with wit and charm, volunteered a few subjects of interest for me related to justice: our current law enforcement environment, the status of sanctuary cities, and other current, popular social issues. Not knowing her views, I told her I would give it a shot.

However, before beginning, it struck me that no group of people in our country were more adversely affected than Native Americans. They were here first, settled their land and homes, and clung to their own culture, traditions, and customs.

According to Lana Leddy Turner, several US government actions impacted Native Americans' social welfare, such as the Indian Appropriations Act of 1871, the Major Crimes Act, the General Allotment Act, and the massacre at Wounded Knee. By the 1800s, most Native Americans had been removed from their homes to reservations, primarily in the West. The US government planned to assimilate them into European American culture. Authorities believed that solutions to "the Indian problem" including reducing Native American autonomy, reeducating their youth, and taking away their land holdings. The results of these policies on Native Americans was generally negative. The Native American culture was suppressed, and the population experienced greater economic hardships. Conflicts between the Native Americans and the government continued.

If the US government could be afforded "redos" in applying social justice, their treatment of Native Americans would rank high on the list. Denying Native Americans citizenship, attempting to eradicate their culture, interfering with the Native Americans' judicial process, and confiscating Native American land were inconceivable injustices. Fortunately, Native Americans have persevered however, but continued to be scarred by social injustices.

Now, let's examine current-day law enforcement and justice.

Law enforcement has recently come under scrutiny regarding the perception of fairness, pertaining to alleged selective enforcement, targeting groups and individuals without due process, excessive force, and unfair treatment in the judicial process. Are these valid points?

As a child I remember the police as professionals who wore nicely pressed uniforms, carried guns, were often friends of families, rode in cars, and protected people. We were taught in home and school to obey our policemen. We experienced little crime—it was a quieter, more peaceful time. Therefore, as children, we had little interaction with the police, except for maybe getting a wave as they drove by.

Reminiscing about my childhood, I quickly realized how things have changed. In those days I had thick, black hair with long sideburns, somewhat Elvis Presley looking; today I'm nearly bald. And today, we're faced with examining perceived problems and concerns regarding our police state.

Whether real or not, it is requiring our police to reflect and conduct internal reviews. As in any occupation, there is and always should be a constant push for improvement and quality performance; law enforcement can be no exception.

It seems that policing has a dilemma in the US. Police have a charter for the maintenance of public order and crime prevention, yet at the same time, the sense of public consensus and cooperation are diminishing. Without positive community relations, police effectiveness will become more challenging to maintain.

What our society seems to want is a police force that ensures safety, prevents crime, and provides human services. This is a difficult and daunting task, considering this hasn't been their purpose historically, and they don't have the manpower, equipment, and training to perform these diverse tasks. Although it appears police are well aware of this demand and are making a concerted effort to establish closer community relations. Time will tell.

According to Former Philadelphia Police Commissioner Charles Ramsey, in an interview with "meet the Press," stated, "There are approximately 18,000 (police) departments in the United States."[30] My first thought was this is a large number of departments and police per the number of actual police abuse cases and criminal convictions. Regardless, law enforcement in our society demands the highest standards. There is little excuse for failure; I doubt we'd want it any other way.

However, we need critical minds when reading and listening to news reports. Today, for example, we're in

30 http://politifact.com//internet/articles/greenberg/How many police departments are in the United States?/0710/2016

a climate of constantly being informed that police are targeting and killing blacks at high rates—and we have a crisis. According to the *National Review*, "far more whites than blacks are killed in confrontations with police," and in 2015, "it was roughly twice as many."

Also, "there are 160 million more whites than blacks in the country." White people make up roughly 62% of the US population, and about 49% of people killed by police officers are white. Of those fatally shot, 24% are African American. Blacks make up 13% of the US population. Based on the numbers, the argument could be made that this is injustice.

However, according to the same *National Review* article, "The elephant in the room, the fundamental to which we must never refer, is propensity toward criminality. It is simply a fact that blacks, and particularly young black men, engage in lawless conduct, very much including violent conduct, at rates (by percentage of population) significantly higher than do other racial or ethnic groups."[31]

"Such a concentration of criminal violence in minority communities means that officers will be disproportionately confronting armed and often resisting suspects in those communities, raising officers' own risk of using lethal force," writes Heather Mac Donald in *The Wall Street Journal.*[32]

31 www.nationalreview.com//article/andrew mccarthy/440361/police shootings black vs white narrative vs fact/2016/09/24
32 ttps://www.daily wire.com/news/bandler/7264/5 statistics you need to know about cops killing/

Peter Moskos, a former Baltimore police officer and criminal justice researcher at John Jay College of Criminal Justice, echoed these ideas in *The New York Times*: "Blacks are three times as likely to be killed by cops as are whites, on a per-capita basis. But part of that is because of crime in predominately black neighborhoods. Blacks are four or five times as likely to be victims of homicides, and they are five times as likely to feloniously kill a cop," he said.

As part of its data effort, The Washington Post tracks the "threat level" of each person who is shot and killed by a police officer: Were they shooting at the officer? Were they threatening the officer? Were they fleeing?

Overall, the majority of the people who have been shot and killed by police officers in 2015 and 2016 were, based on publicly available evidence, armed with a weapon and attempting to attack the officer or someone else. The study also determined whether officers are more likely to shoot and kill someone who is unarmed, if the shooting happened in a high-crime area. They concluded that is not the case.

"There's too much violence in the black community" former New York City Mayor Rudy Giuliani told CBS's *Face the Nation*. He added, "If you want to deal with this on the black side, you've got to teach your children to be respectful to the police, and you've got to teach your children that the real danger to them is not the police, the real danger to them 99 out of 100 times, 9,900 out of 10,000 times are other black kids who are going to kill them. That's the way they're going to die."[33]

Turns out Giuliani was close to the mark. According to FBI numbers from 2014, about 90% of black homicide victims were killed by other black people. That same year the white-on-white murder rate—homicides in which a white person was killed by another white—was 82%.

Overwhelmingly, the victims of black crime are black people. In her book *The War on Cops*, Heather Mac Donald relates that only 4% of black homicide victims are killed in police interactions. If African American parents were really having "the talk" that's pertinent to protecting their children, it would have to involve the reality that those children are overwhelmingly more likely to be shot by other black youths. The police are having "police involved" confrontations with young black men largely because black communities demand police protection—and understandably so.

Also, we often hear that white cops are preying on black men. In too many "police-involved" incidents, such as the tragic one in Charlotte, the officers themselves are black. The news narrative doesn't hold.

It seems that if there's a police-involved shooting, we assume it's racially motivated. Why? Why do some also assume that because blacks are shot, policing is racial and unjust? Why is race questioned in police actions before the facts are determined? Why do we often have protests and demonstrations, some violent, when police are acquitted by

33 https://www.cbsnews.com/news/face-the-nation-transcripts-july-10-2016-rawlings-johnson-bratton-brooks-cummings-giuliani/

a jury and the law? Why is there is so much anger and hate regarding a particular police case, rather than on the bigger picture and larger number of people shooting and killing each other?

Chicago is a good example of this rampant violence. In 2017, there was 650 murders, a drop from 771 in 2016, and 2,785 shootings in Chicago. On average, a person is shot every two hours and 17 minutes and murdered every 12 and a half hours. Most of the murder victims are black, killed by other blacks. During this same timeframe, 18 people have been killed by police in the Chicago area, and in the city itself, police have killed 10 people. The vast majority of these police killings fit into the category of justified homicide.[34]

We hear little in the news regarding the violence and homicides in Chicago or any other inner cities. What we hear is constant blaming of police, and avoidance of the necessary actions to promote change. As long as this rhetoric and shouting continues, without facing the facts and reality, little change will occur. It hasn't in Chicago.

The point here is that we shouldn't excuse or ignorantly jump on the bandwagon with those who use law enforcement officers as scapegoats for their own agendas or for criminal activity. Neither should we tolerate those who abuse officers performing their duties. Furthermore, we shouldn't applaud and prod the small minority who have

---

34 *http://cnn.com//internet/news/park/Chicago police count fewer murders in 2017, but still 650 people were killed/01/012018*

little character, respect, or intelligence, and act with anger to instigate and hurt.

I can't help wondering if the recent actions of a few individuals and groups is a fair depiction of our law enforcement in general. Are these recent protests of police brutality and injustice based on fact and truthful media reporting? As a former NFL quarterback recently stated, "There are bodies in the street and people are getting paid leave and getting away with murder."[35] Truthful media, yes—this is a direct quote. Based on facts, no.

A study last year by Harvard Economics Professor Roland Fryer, who is black, concluded that for the Houston police department, "On the most extreme use of force—officer-involved shootings—we find no racial differences in either the raw data or when contextual factors are taken into account."[36]

In John Lott's article "NFL Kneeling Protests on False Claims and Misleading Media Reports," he indicates that "four national databases of crime statistics representing confrontations between police and civilians in many parts of the US ... did find that blacks were more likely than whites to be treated with some lower level of force by police during confrontations—such as being handcuffed, pushed to the ground, or pepper sprayed." And, he also wrote that this "is a legitimate issue that merits further study. But it's not the

35 https://theguardian.com//news/ameerhasan loggins/We can't hear Colin Kaepernick any more. He's being drowned out by noise/09/27/2017
36 https://law.yale.edu/system/files/area/workshop/leo/leo16_fryer.pdf

same as saying racist white cops are ... 'getting away with murder' of African Americans."[37]

Also, regarding police relations with the black community, "a 2016 Quinnipiac University poll found that blacks strongly support the cops in their neighborhoods—68 percent approve compared to just 25 percent who disapprove. That rating is 11 percent higher than blacks give the New York City Police Department as a whole, where perceptions are far more likely to be influenced by media reports. Among all American adults, 50 percent see police as friends, while 6 percent see police as enemies and 42 percent don't think of police as friends or enemies."[38]

Mr. Lott further writes, "The media have helped create a biased perception that is far from reality on police shootings. In a new study, the Crime Prevention Research Center finds that when a white officer kills a suspect, the media usually mention the race of the officer. This is rarely true when the officer is black. As a result, many people incorrectly believe the police are racist. But when it comes to the cops who African Americans deal with personally, they often have a different view."

Per Lott, data from the Department of Justice "also shows blacks don't hesitate to reach out to police and report crime. Indeed, from 2008 to 2012, blacks were actually *more likely* than whites, Hispanics, or Asians to report

---

37 htttp://foxnews.com//internet/news/john lott/NFL kneeling protests based on false claims and misleading media reports/10/21/2017/
38 http://poll.qu.edu/internet/poll/Quinnipiac/Poll/Oct11,2016

violent crimes committed against them to the police."

The statistics show that "blacks were 9 percentage more likely than whites (54 percent to 45 percent) to report a crime to the police. Blacks are 16 percent more likely than Hispanics and 12 percent more likely than Asians." Furthermore, "It's not just that blacks report more crime because they experience more of it. This higher rate of reporting even holds true in areas where other groups face higher violent crime rates than blacks do."

"More importantly," says Lott, "this trust in local community police appears to be well-placed. This is because despite what ... others falsely claims, white police officers aren't killing defenseless blacks just because they can. Blacks also are a smaller percentage of people killed by police than the black share of murderers and other violent criminals."

"Without a doubt, it should be a national law enforcement goal to reduce police shootings. To do so will require changes in our law enforcement procedures, training, and operations."

During trying times and when dealing with difficult, sensitive issues, it's important to find truth, to think for ourselves, and to keep open minds. Unfortunately, in today's society too many are unwilling to seek or accept truth. Recent incidents in our country demonstrate that this attitude and behavior can be dangerous.

In our communities, we all have a responsibility to

preserve the peace and ensure each other's safety. Law enforcement cannot effectively perform their duties without the citizenry's trust and support.

Imagine anti-police extremists, if law enforcement was nonexistent during natural disasters, demonstrations, and heightened security across our nation. The hypocrisy would be overbearing. There would be little peace or safety and indescribable destruction and violence. A minority-abusing police force and instilling hate and violence won't change the need for law and order.

How about a national campaign reinforcing this idea 'We respect and support our police, and hold each and every person accountable for his or her actions"? The police need our respect, as each of us wants to be respected. This respect for each other will lead us to a feeling of confidence and trust rather than fear and intimidation.

It's crucial that law enforcement listens to their respective community's voices with open minds and takes opportunities to increase partnerships. It appears they are committed to this. Can changes be made so policing becomes more collaborative and transparent in the administration of justice? Probably so.

As in all occupations, new technology and training is paramount. Years ago, I was reminded of this daily, while working as an intern for the State's Attorney in New Haven, Connecticut. He would often describe the importance of technology and training in local and federal law enforcement—initial training, follow-up training, annual training, etc.

All law enforcement agencies need to conduct recurrent and up-to-date training. This training is critical and must be taken seriously. The training must stay abreast with current threats, technology, and the daily environment. The education must also include cultural, diversity, and crisis management training, to ensure that police standards and misconduct are well understood and that all officers will be held accountable. Those unable to complete the training need to be removed.

Equally important to ongoing training, according to the article "The Case for Procedural Justice: Fairness as a Crime Prevention Tool," is procedural justice, which the authors state is the "frequently practiced but often overlooked approach that has increasingly been identified by researchers as an evidence-based and cost-effective way to reduce crime." Per the article, procedural justice "describes the idea that how individuals regard the justice system is tied more to the perceived fairness of the *process* and how they were treated rather than to the perceived fairness of the *outcome*."[39]

The article goes on to state,

"Underlying procedural justice is the idea that the criminal justice system must constantly be

---

39 http://cops.usdoj.gov//internet/newsletter/Emily Gold &Melissa Bradley/ *The Case for Procedural Justice: Fairness as a Crime Prevention Tool/ September 2013/*

demonstrating its legitimacy to the public it serves. If the public ceases to view its justice system as legitimate, dire consequences ensue. Put simply, people are more likely to comply with the law and cooperate with law enforcement efforts when they feel the system and its actors are legitimate."[40]

Additionally, we need to continue to work on hiring common-sense diversity in our police forces. No one who is unqualified and/or ineligible should ever be hired. This issue regarding hiring practices isn't new for law enforcement. The current underrepresentation of African Americans, Hispanics, and Asians in policing exists for many reasons.

In the early 1990s, while assigned at the Pentagon, the Deputy Assistant Secretary of the Air Force, Air Staff officers, and I, pursued a project to recruit more minorities into aviation careers. The Air Force at that time was visibly underrepresented in minority pilots. After talking with numerous students, and attending career days and colleges throughout the country, one observation was clear, most of these students were not interested. There were many reasons, different and similar, but the bottom line was, they were not interested. I understood then, its exceedingly difficult to recruit individuals into certain careers depending upon the time and environment. Forced recruitment is not a good idea for all parties involved. Law enforcement may

40 http://cops.usdoj.gov//internet/newsletter/Emily Gold & Melissa Bradley/The Case for Procedural Justice: Fairness as a Crime Prevention Tool/September 2013/

experience this similar challenge for the foreseeable future.

Regardless, it's imperative that we continue working to recruit young adults, as well as ensuring that hiring practices are fair and equitable. It would also be beneficial if police recruitment mirrored military recruitment, with recruiters developing relationships with community organizations, schools, universities, and churches. Our current law enforcement image may be unfair, and it needs to be evaluated. Until then, recruitment will continue to be challenging.

A community's trust in their police is vital, particularly in areas with higher percentages of minority residents. With an absence of minority representation in law enforcement, trust can erode. To gain trust, a police force must earn it by demonstrating excellence in all they do.

Throughout America, police have their communities' trust. Today, they must maintain it, and reengineer themselves in areas where there is doubt.

Also, language barriers can stymie policing. Officers able to speak the same language as their community are advantageous, providing immediate response and resolution and eliminating the need for translators.

Officers of different races may react differently to certain situations because of their familiarity with the culture, language, and people. They may be able to better differentiate the community pulse, and the behaviors of the people living in it.

Fortunately, police realize the need for staff diversity. However, a diverse staff alone won't automatically improve a community's image of its police. Leading by example, with openness and a caring attitude, under the law, will ultimately gain police their community's trust and legitimacy.

Our law enforcement community needs city-by-city review and changes made where necessary. Whatever changes occur, paramount is the community's ability to trust their police, feel respected as citizens, and know justice is served equitably.

The need for Comprehensive Immigration Reform

America also has an immigration system that has been inept for years and is in violation of the Constitution, with no clear policy or vision. This issue is very important to American citizens, immigrants, and their families. Now is the time to build a comprehensive, well-thought-out, bipartisan immigration policy, centered on our Constitution and providing law-abiding immigrants the privilege of becoming Americans.

Immigration has been a contentious issue in the US from its earliest days. In 1798, President John Adams signed the Alien and Sedition Acts, giving the government authority to arrest foreigners who were perceived to oppose the federal government, and to deport them. Later, when Thomas Jefferson became president, the Acts were repealed.

Throughout US history, immigration policies have

widely varied. We've had a centralized immigration policy for the whole country, the banning of individuals and certain groups of individuals, a national quota system (which has since been abolished), the beginning of border patrol and customs enforcement, preference given to skilled workers and family members, and more recently, diversity initiatives.

We continue to be a divided nation regarding immigration. On one hand, immigrants have provided labor, been patriotic and proud citizens, and provided different cultures blending into our nation. On the other hand, some native-born Americans have seen these people as different, troublemakers, security risks, and absorbing labor in the competitive job market.

Our immigration policies need change and reform. Processing should include specific and clear requirements, be streamlined, be thorough, and include background checks.

Currently, per FreeAdvice® Legal, "the approval time to become a US citizen varies by person and location. ... it can take anywhere from 5 to 8 months between application and interview. If you live in an area with heavy immigrant populations, it is not unusual to wait 2 years or more to become a US citizen."[41]

A goal should be established to process all immigrants in six months or less. In doing so, our government should determine ways to streamline processing. Furthermore, our

41 https://immigration-law.freeadvice.com/immigration-law/citizenship/us_citizen_filing_length.htm

government should retain the right to deny any individual the right to citizenship, based on transparent criteria. Let's remember while dreading through this emotional issue, immigrating to any country is a privilege not a right. The US government has the right to determine who is allowed into America, and who is not. For many, this truth has been overlooked.

It isn't just or sensible to have immigrants who are attending school, working, and being good citizens to have to wait for citizenship. This seems easier than we have made it. Although the world is a much different place than it was a few decades ago.

We can't seem to develop national immigration policies and therefore have found ourselves with defiant local government thumbing their noses at the federal government, declaring themselves sanctuary cities as a means of justice. The federal government, in turn, is threatening to withhold federal funding to sanctuary cities. Because of this occurrence, Americans are losing trust in the government, sanctuary communities, and immigrants themselves. We're losing trust in one another.

Rather than do the tough work together and overhaul our nation's failing immigration system with new laws and protections, we have become more divided, antagonistic, and content to ignore the necessity. The issue isn't a simple one. It involves numerous legal and constitutional questions, and people's lives. Whether it is decided to pursue one piece of immigration policy at a time or overhaul the entire program – let's get started.

Our attempts to reform the immigration program remind me of sprinters competing in a race and the official repeatedly blowing the whistle for false starts and the runners required to regroup at the starting line. Congress is currently wrestling with what to do regarding the Deferred Action for Childhood Arrivals, DACA, Chain and Migration, by which one immigrant can sponsor family members to come to the US, border security, and the current Lottery System of Immigration. The latter is a program that awards visas to screened individuals from nations with lower levels of immigration into the US. Even though these programs are significantly important and need to be resolved, they are not all inclusive of the work needed to be done.

Another issue is the establishment of sanctuary cities. What are sanctuary cities? In the US, they're cities that provide safe haven to undocumented immigrants and limit its cooperation with federal law enforcement officials' efforts to enforce the immigration law. Involved cities want to manage their own immigration policies and maintain their judicial process regarding immigrants, without federal government intrusion. The federal government feels they have the authority and responsibility to intercede in illegal immigration affairs and criminal activity.

The feds have information, intelligence, and a broader communication network daily reaching around the world.

State and local law enforcement are less enhanced. The feds' primary goal is to ensure our country remains secure and safe. This is a difficult enough task, without having cities with less information and intelligence harboring potential criminals.

Sanctuary cities aren't a long-term solution to American immigration, and for that matter, they benefit few in the short term. Undocumented immigrants committing crimes will be prosecuted in sanctuary cities like any citizen. So what's the purpose? The cities and some states versus the federal government? It's like watching 8-year-olds playing checkers to determine who wins the most red or black pieces.

It's doubtful the law-abiding immigrant feels any safer and secure in a sanctuary city than in a city that is not one. The feds' concern is that the criminal or potential criminals do have a safety net, a sanctuary. Numerous cases show how these people were protected while committing one or more felonies.

The article, "Do Undocumented Immigrants Overuse Government Benefits?" provides an overview of the types of benefits undocumented immigrants can or cannot receive: "Unauthorized immigrants are ineligible for most major federally-funded programs. ... [They] are not eligible to receive Social Security benefits even though many contribute to the system." However, if the Deferred Action for Childhood Arrivals (DACA) program lasts, it will permit participants who pay into Social Security eventual benefit payouts. Additionally, some federal programs serve those in need, regardless of immigration status. These programs include school meal programs, nutrition for women, infants, and children, and Emergency Medicaid.

It is important to note that "many unauthorized immigrants have dependent children or a spouse who are citizens and who may qualify for public benefits. About three quarters of children of undocumented immigrants are citizens. ... Therefore, although undocumented immigrants are ineligible for most benefits, their households often receive support."[42]

The questions can be asked: Are states and localities abusing immigration law and programs regarding benefits to undocumented immigrants? Have they made decisions to act upon perceived injustice, disregarding the law? Have undocumented immigrants themselves found loopholes to abuse government benefits? What should be done regarding undocumented immigrants who require public assistance and depend on taxpayer help? Are sanctuary cities, which are now "winning" the most checkers, more apt to ignore the federal government regardless of the law?

The entire state of California became a sanctuary state on January 1, 2018, which makes sense since undocumented immigrants make up an estimated 10% of California's workforce. Although California officials

42 http://econofact.org//internet/articles/tara watson/Do Undocumented Immigrants Overuse Government Benefits?/03/28/2017

claim this workforce is essential to their state economy, and probably so, what's happening to many of these poor immigrants? Many factories are breaking wage laws. There is wage theft by employers, and inhumane and unsafe working conditions. Laborers are being paid under the table and paying no taxes, and studies show immigration lowers wages for skilled native workers and prior immigrants. The American people hear little about this.

In the business of employing undocumented immigrants, the employer continues to grow richer, while the laborer ceiling is minimum wage or less. Not a pretty picture for a self-professed progressive state, yet California continues its outcry for fairness and justice.

Our country needs a new and more efficient immigration program, one that abides by the law, is just and fair for all immigrants, and continues to ensure our nation's security and safety.

Is Poverty in America a Social Justice Concern

"Overcoming poverty is not a gesture of
charity. It is the protection of a fundamental
human right, the right to dignity and a decent
life." –Nelson Mandela, Former President of
South Africa

I wondered for days if in America we consider poverty a social justice issue. Poverty is rarely found in the most popular social issues of our time, and even more so, is seldom discussed. It's as if, Americans realize poverty exists, however rationalize it as inevitable and unsolvable. This is my perception.

What Americans may not know, is the extent of poverty, in our country and the actions being taken, or not, to decrease it and improve the poor's quality of life. Unfortunately, poverty is not easy to define and measure. When considering many factors, to include: wages, family size, cost of living, housing costs, expenses incurred by the working poor, make it difficult to determine who and how many Americans live in poverty. However, according to the U.S. Census Bureau, using household income, our nations poverty rate in 2016 was 12.7 percent, with 40.6 million people in poverty. The total population of the U.S. was 319.9 million. The number of people without health insurance in 2016 was 28.1 million people. As defined by the Office of Management and Budget, the weighted average poverty threshold for a family of four in 2016 was $24, 563.

Also released in September 2017 by the U.S. Census Bureau are the following U.S. Poverty Statistics: "The U.S. poverty rate has been fairly static over the past 30 years. The rate in 1989 was 12.8% and the average for the past thirty years is 13.5%. The child poverty rate in 2016 was 18.0%, therefore about one in five children were in a poverty status. This is a disturbing poverty statistic to many Americans because children are helpless to influence their living conditions. Many of these children come from single parent families. The single mother poverty rate was 26.6%. Adults that work full time had a low poverty rate of 2.2%. There were 46.1 million adults between the ages of 18 and 64 that were not working. They accounted for 62% of the working age in poverty. The total not working group had a poverty rate of 30.5%. The educational level attained by individuals had a dramatic impact on poverty. 24.8% of adults over 25 years old without a high school diploma are in poverty versus 4.5% for those with a college degree."

According to Ron Haskins of the Brookings Institution, testifying before Congress on June 5, 2012, "Young people can virtually assure that they and their families will avoid poverty if they follow three elementary rules for success – complete at least a high school education, work full time, and wait until age 21 and get married before having a baby. Based on an analysis of Census data, people who followed all three of these rules has only a 2 percent chance of being in poverty and a 72 percent chance of joining the middle class (identified as above $55, 000)."[43]

The above illustrates that the poverty rate has remained relatively stable, though without visible improvement over time. The U.S. has not done a very good job of fighting poverty and it appears a problem no one knows how to solve. Alissa Walker, Curbed news, in her article, Why isn't homelessness seen as a national crisis? quoted United Nations investigators in their U.N. report: "The American Dream is rapidly becoming the American Illusion, as the

43 https://www.finance.senate.gov/doc/Ron Haskins/06052012

U.S. ...now has the lowest social mobility of any of the rich countries. The US is one of the richest, most powerful, and technologically innovative countries; but neither wealth not its power not its technology is being harnessed to address the situation in which 40 million people continue to live in poverty," wrote Philip Alston, a United Nations Special Rapporteur on extreme poverty and human rights. The investigators also reported the United States has the highest child poverty rates in the developed world.[44]

This concern for human life demands nothing less than our national commitment towards ending this social injustice. For far too long this commitment has not existed.

Our society is impacted by poverty and vice versa. Our justice system is responsible for the oversight and enforcement of laws and policies governing the poor. Therefore, poverty may be one of the most important, yet overlooked social justice issues of our time.

What we know is demonstrations, social and political advocates, local charities, and government action alone will not cut and sustain poverty levels. Even though each initiative is positive, well intentioned and should be continued, they require support. For example, the U.S. government in the mid–1960s spent millions of dollars on poverty with some good results and others as failures. The poverty rates during this timeframe fluctuated between a little over 10 percent to near 15 percent. The welfare

44 http://www.curbed.com//internet/article/AlissaWalker/why isn't homelessness seen as a national crisis?/02012018

program was a temporary aide for some in poverty but not a long term solution to a multifaceted and difficult problem.

The Rev. Martin Luther King Jr.'s "Poor Peoples Campaign" began in Washington D.C., and was an example of a valiant effort through peaceful demonstration to raise awareness of poverty in America. Unfortunately, many activists disagreed with Rev. King's peaceful movement and chose other more aggressive approaches towards their goals. A few weeks after the initial demonstrations in Washington D.C. began, on November 22, 1963, President Kennedy, a staunch supporter of the movement, was assassinated. Soon after, the momentum and passion of the demonstrators waned, the movement withered away. It was over.

So how do we decrease poverty, possibly in half to 6 percent a sustainable rate by the year 2025? This poverty level is realistic and achievable. A much lower rate cannot be. Too many variables and categories of people in poverty exist to believe we can alleviate all poverty with a few solutions, and expect one solution to work for all. When dealing with this issue, we need to consider and use current and historical data identifying those in poverty by race, marital status, employment, those with disability, where they live, and their education levels. In other words, it's also important to know who have remained in poverty over a given time and who have escaped poverty, and why/how?

This data can assist our nation-wide attention and

commitment to deal with the problem of poverty. Many federal government agencies either administer programs that assist low income families or compile useful poverty data. There are also many local and state groups fighting poverty. Social support and job training programs exist throughout America, although in some cases need to be expanded and improved. These services need to ensure the poor unemployed who are able to work are connected to the job market and full-time employment. The Department of Human Services, the state's social service agency, actively promotes community service, early education, housing/community development, senior and adult services and workforce development. Most of these agencies have been in place for decades, and yet poverty lingers. Nevertheless, they are productive and needed.

It has been gratifying over the past few years to see more disadvantaged people, elderly, minimally educated, and possibly at-risk young adults employed in retail and grocery stores, hospitals, restaurants, malls, in construction work, fitness centers, and various other occupations. I'm assuming many of these jobs are full time and at least minimum wage or higher. Also, it is my observation many of these employees have been unemployed, in/out of poverty, and have returned to the workforce. I believe this is what most Americans want, if only given the opportunity. If so, this is a positive trend.

It seems the necessary organizations and support and services are in place to deal with the problem of poverty.

It may be time to challenge and hold states themselves responsible for their poverty levels. State politicians, business leaders, educators, social servants and advocates, clergy, and other state groups and leaders need to come together committed to establishing and achieving their own goals. The federal government needs to continue their involvement with funding, support, and legislation, if or when necessary. The states should accept responsibility for their poor and be held accountable.

Each state is different in size, overall population, poverty rates, unemployment rates, and demographics, and have experienced different results fighting poverty. For example, according to the Census Bureau's Supplemental Poverty Measure, California, with 12% of the American population has the highest poverty rate of all states where nearly one out of five residents are poor. According to Kerry Jackson, "Why is liberal California the poverty capital of America?" Los Angeles Times, Jan 14, 2018, "California state and local governments spent nearly $958 billion from 1992 through 2015 on public welfare programs, including cash – assistance payments, vendor payments and other public welfare, according to Census Bureau. California is home to about one in three of the nation's welfare recipients. The generous spending, then, has not only failed to decrease poverty; it actually seems to have made it worse." California's enormous bureaucracy and welfare mindset has been a long-term failure "while paying little or no political price." The state's poverty problem is unlikely to improve while policy makers resist pro-work reforms and remain unwilling to change their political stubbornness.[45] Regardless of California politics, this laissez faire approach to the problem of poverty has been and continues to be a disservice to the state's poor.

These facts, and California alone, clearly impact our nation's ability to substantially lower overall poverty levels. It's as if in our optimism to begin fixing the problem of poverty we are behind and handicapped from the start. If there are future demonstrations and activism, the movement should begin in Sacramento and touch every state to Washington, D.C. Not in honor of Rev. King, but to carry on and complete his work finding justice for the poor.

Unlike California, many states, principally Wisconsin, Michigan, and Virginia have initiated welfare reform, along with the federal government. Stressing strong work requirements has resulted in welfare rolls decreasing and millions of former aid recipients entering the labor force. Wisconsin's poverty rate in 2015 was 9.7% down from 10.8% in 2014, according to the Wisconsin Poverty Measure (WPM) and was the lowest rate recorded in the past nine years. The WPM reported "the drop in the poverty rate was aided by 70,000 additional jobs gained in the state between January 2014 and November 2015." Virginia's 2015 poverty rate was 11.2% a direct result of higher educational levels and a 4.4% unemployment rate.

---

45 www.latimes.com/opinion/op-ed/la-oe-jackson-california-poverty-20180114-story.html

After examining poverty data and observing government success dealing with poverty, it is evident people are more likely to avoid poverty if they are educated, have full-time jobs, and have balanced family lives. Therefore, creating well compensated jobs and providing improved access to education and training opportunities, and ensuring accessible social support and health related programs and services, should be each states priorities. And of course, the economy has a great effect on poverty. States have little control over fluctuations in the economy and should establish their goals and programs to withstand any economic turbulence.

Hopefully, our country will never stray from the ideals of hard work, initiative, motivation and to using our God given talents and abilities to become the best we can be. And, that all people should have equality of opportunity. That as Americans we are not mislead believing the problem of poverty lies with those fortunate who have worked, prospered economically and advanced in life. They are neither the cause or solution to the poverty in our nation. The plight of the poor has not improved for decades because we have either chosen to ignore them, or like California, the state's leadership has mismanaged the issue without accountability or oversight.

However, the rising inequality of opportunity and wealth in America is certainly a social justice issue and one requiring our attention. In a recent article by Ivana Kottasova, "The 1% grabbed 82% of all wealth created in

2017." The Oxfam International, using data from Credit Suisse's Global Wealth Databook, reported more than $8 of every $10 of wealth created last year went to the richest 1%," and "estimates that the bottom 50% of the world's population saw no increase in wealth. The report also highlights the detrimental effects of gender inequality."[46]

Now days, I'm a little skeptical and occasionally critical of reports, surveys, and polls. Regarding Oxfam's report, let's assume it is closely accurate. The U.S. is a contributor to this global economic reality, and good reason why women are now demonstrating for gender equality. This inequality issue is one issue most Americans agree on, but more action is needed.

There are daily accusations and stories of gender discrimination encompassing women in various careers throughout America. In many of these cases there is little reasonable explanation or rationale. This wage inequity occurs primarily in the private sector where there are no wage systems and employers have salary discretion. Where males and females are performing the same duties/services and all other employee data is similar will we begin to eventually see wage equality? What is it going to take to correct this injustice? Would equal pay also attract more women to the workforce, a group we are in dire need of? And if so, would this favorably impact our nations poverty levels?

---

46 *http://CNN Money//internet/articles/Ivana Kottasova/The 1% grabbed 82% of all wealth created in 2017/ 01222018*

"It's Not Fair": How Can We Deal with Social Challenges in Today's Culture?

Throughout our history, when Americans have wanted something bad enough, they achieved it. I have hope and faith in our country that one day we will come together state by state, city by city, in each neighborhood, to assist and care for the poor. There are no excuses, or should we project any blame. With optimism let's remember the many Americans from our teens to the elderly who have assisted the poor, made significant contributions to fighting poverty, and who have put their service to this issue above themselves. Each of us has a responsibility to care for one another ... if only we are willing.

The Story of Joe, The Barber

Joe owned a two-seat barber shop in the impoverished side of a Capital city. He was a good barber, gregarious, a talker, who seemed to know everybody. He had immigrated from Italy with his wife Josephine, and once settled began their business from scratch. It was an extremely difficult period financially with the addition of their first child.

As the years progressed, business steadily improved to a six day a week, nine hour a day schedule. Josephine began doing the accounting and occasionally cutting hair in the second chair. While Joe, more fluent in English did most the talking, Josephine, would listen and glow with the "most beautiful and genuine smile", the customers often repeated. She had a devout admiration for her husband and loved being with people. What no one ever knew was Josephine did not like cutting hair — she did it for her family.

She always felt fortunate to have the barbershop and see her husband happy each day.

With Josephine's help and their business prospering Joe found time to pursue his passion, working with leather. In a dark, small, dilapidated shed behind the barber shop was the smell of leather and cigar smoke — it was a smell few would forget. This is where Joe restored and repaired leather items. He had shoes, bags, and coats hanging from walls, on shelves, and on the floor. Joe would restring and restore ball gloves and athletic shoes for the kids, mostly poor, who resided in the neighborhood. He would do it for little or no cost. Each baseball season in the spring they would be lined up at his door. The kids loved talking with Joe and the smell of the "dug out" as they referred to it.

As the long weeks began to wear on Joe, he decided to hire a new barber full time. Three individuals immediately applied, all with barber experience. Joe hired Ernie, a black middle-aged man, who for some time had been in and out of jobs. Ernie had a family of four with two teen age children. Ernie, like Joe, was a good barber and enjoyed people. One day he asked Joe, with customers in the shoproom, why he was hired. Joe stated, "because Josephine told me to!" The entire room broke out in laughter.

Ernie became as popular a barber as Joe and together they made a comfortable living. Ernie continued barbering well after both his children graduated college. As Ernie tells it, "It was something my wife and I never thought possible. Our children now have opportunities I could only have dreamed of."

Joe, with Ernie's help, renovated the "dug out" and opened his leather business, part time. Josephine quit cutting hair though stayed busy with the business finances. She is now spending more time with their child and tending to family matters.

> "Poverty will exist where people are self –
> serving and apathetic; it will be stymied in
> cultures where love lives and insistence to
> helping people out of poverty." –Gene Matera

Quality Education for all Students

Lastly, how are our students doing educationally versus other countries? For some time we've known that the answer is "not very well." The US is a superpower and a highly technological society. So why are we lagging behind?

According to Drew Desilver of the Pew Research Center, "U.S. students continue to rank around the middle of the pack, and behind many other advanced industrial nations."[47]

The fact that we continue to rank low is nothing new; it's where we've always been.

The Programme for International Student Assessment (PISA) measures many skills among 15–year–olds around the world, including math, reading, and science. The 2015

47 http://pewresearch.org//internet/news/desilver/U.S. students'
academic achievement still lags that of their peers in many other
countries/02/15/2017

PISA results "placed the US an unimpressive 38th out of 71 countries in math and 24th in science. Among the 35 members of the Organization for Economic Cooperation and Development, which sponsors the PISA initiative, the US ranked 30th in math and 19th in science."[48]

As the US continues struggling to provide quality K–12 education for all children, and compete globally, again we're faced with division. We're faced with parents' rights and desires versus laws, policies, and funding. The states responsibilities for their education programs versus federal mandates. Family access for school choice. And, the future role of unions in public education.

The US has passed numerous legislation regarding publication education since the early 1960s. Much of this federal law has failed to raise the quality of education for students. Currently Common Core State Standards prevails. Will School Choice and Education Opportunity Act (SCAEOA) be the next law?

Early in our nation's history, lawmakers passed the 10th Amendment to the Constitution which made education a state function. The federal government has always had a minor role in education but wasn't involved in education legislation until the 1960s. President Johnson's administration, and the "Great Society" program, increased federal involvement. This same involvement has intensified

---

48 http://pew research.org//internet/news/desilver/U.S. students 'academic achievement still lags that of their peers in many other countries/02/15/2017

since then, with policymakers and politicians constantly talking education reform.

Along with more federal involvement in education policy, the government allocates funding to school districts that follow federal guidelines. Schools are also administered and financed by their communities and state government. According to the U.S. Department of Education, "the funding for the Department of Education in 2017, was $69.4 billion, an increase of $1.3 billion, or 2 percent, over the 2016 enacted level, adjusted for comparability."[49]

States are primarily responsible for the maintenance and operation of their public schools. States are involved in the establishment, selection, and regulation of curriculum, teaching methods, and instructional materials in their schools. Each state has different standards and policies that impact the quality of education offered.

Therefore, we currently have a K–12 educational program that involves the federal government legislating, each state developing different policies and standards, and federal, state, and local governments providing funds. The teachers' unions add to this bureaucracy.

It's obvious that government bureaucracy hasn't succeeded in benefitting our children's education and needs to be streamlined.

However, the government and school funding aren't the

---

49 http://ED.gov/ budget17/budget–factsheet/2017 Budget – US
Department of Education/

main reasons the US is lagging, and many of our students are unprepared for college and adult life in general.

What quality education means to each of us can be very different. Is it more time spent in school? Having the best teachers? Access to good schools? Strengthening the rigor and relevancy of classes? Curriculum focusing on technical education? A need for a track system? A focus on math, science, and communications skills? Decreasing class sizes? More emphasis on the arts? More or fewer extracurricular activities? Language skills? Less mandatory testing and more teaching time?

There are many possible answers and combinations. What's most fair to each child is that they have the opportunity to attend good schools. Many minority, and poor students in particular, don't have the same opportunities as their peers. Funded school choice would go a long way in providing these children equal opportunity. Schools consistently not providing quality K–12 education should be required to improve and meet/exceed standards or be closed. Parents and their children attending these schools have the right to voice, "It's not fair." It isn't.

Our current educational system, beginning in the middle school years, has many curriculum options. These myriad options foster an ambiguous sense of what we want our students to learn, with the exception of the high achievers, who will succeed regardless.

Is this what we want? Or can other policy solutions fit

into our educational system?

For example, the Germans tell their students what they need to learn and that they must do well in certain subjects to continue on to college. They also have a very good vocational track program and a white-collar career track for those students not going to college—the students have a choice. According to a *U.S. News & World Report* article, "Best Countries for Education," Germany ranks number four globally in 2017.

We often wonder why many Asian students outperform all others. It's often a joke among students themselves, and our society writes it off as "a cultural thing." However, it is much more than their culture when many Asian countries, poor and affluent, are succeeding.

According to Marc Tucker, President and CEO of the National Center on Education and Economy, "In places like Hong Kong, Shanghai, South Korea, and Vietnam, fewer than 5 percent of 15- year-old students performed below the basic-proficiency level in reading, mathematics, and science. But, in the United States, 12 percent—half a million students—fell below the same level in all three subjects."[50] In these few East Asian countries, all with 5% or fewer failing students, it's apparent that they're teaching to each student while also not sacrificing the success of the average or high achievers.

Both Vietnam and Latvia, low socioeconomic countries,

50 *http://theatlantic.com//internet/articles/tucker/Asian Countries Take the U.S. to School/02/29/2016*

"have far smaller percentages of low-performing students than the US." Therefore, poverty can affect a family's educational opportunities, though it's not a primary reason for lack of success.

Tucker also noted one significant difference: "in the American system, as students start to fall behind, they find it harder and harder to comprehend what is going on in class and fall farther behind as they go through the years. Their morale sinks, their embarrassment rises, they stop coming to school, and then they drop out."[51]

My observation is that many of these students try to remain in school, but eventually fail and then quit. This spiral can span their entire high-school careers without immediate intervention and consistent guidance and support. It's imperative that we keep all of our students in school and prevent student dropouts—no dropout rate is acceptable.

The Asian countries take a different approach to struggling students: "they start from a commitment to the idea that all students can and will meet high standards as they progress through the years," based on the assumption that all children can learn at high levels.

Each one of these countries and Japan have unique policies and programs to ensure student success. As Mr. Tucker notes, it is "the expectation and insistence that all students will meet high standards," including disadvantaged

51 http://theatlantic.com//internet/articles/Tucker/Asian Countries Take the U.S. to School/02/29/2016

students, that is the key to their success. This policy is fully specified and agreed upon by each country.

A few years ago, the high school where I taught was receiving its six-year Western Association of Schools and Colleges (WASC) review. The team of state officials visited to review our school action plan and observe our ability to demonstrate evidence of acceptable student achievement and school improvement.

When the team completed their school-wide review, they out briefed the entire staff. They had numerous positives regarding our plan and vision, the staff, our students, and our community. Overall, we exceeded standards. No surprise—this is a top-notch school. However, I remember a suggestion they provided as they concluded: that we should challenge our students more, raise our expectations of them, and increase the rigor in our teaching. They stated that the teachers and students were capable of this next step.

I remembered thinking, how very true. How do we accomplish this? How do we teach to each student's potential? Often, it's too easy to lower expectations for students in lieu of meeting standards and being satisfied.

Based on over 18 years of teaching, I estimate that approximately 30% of graduating K-12 students are unprepared to attend universities. Of this same group, approximately 15% of graduates have no realistic goals after tossing their caps and receiving their diplomas. This roughly 15 percent of graduates are neither employed nor enrolled in college.[52] For the students intending to pursue vocational trades, they had little practical and hand-on education and training.

This observation is derived from teaching at three high-quality high schools.

To elevate students to the next level of learning and ensuring their success seemed so right. I looked forward to seeing this teaching and learning materialize. However, the necessary changes would require a completely new mindset for state officials, district and administrative staffs, parents, teachers, and the students themselves. And this change must begin at the elementary school level.

A few possible solutions can be explored to ensure competence in the US K–12 education system:

- Considering a year-round calendar while maintaining the standard 180 days (with Saturday school for students as needed).
- Alternately, exploring adding school days to the current 180-day calendar. Students in most developed nations spend many more days per year in school than in the US. For instance, children in China attend school 260 days, Australians students are in the classroom 220 days, and Russian schools operate 211 days per year.

52 https://www.usnews.com/education/blogs/high-school-notes/2012/08/22/high-school-students-not-prepared-for-college-career

- Using school time to emphasize academic work instead of extracurricular activities.
- Assessing and intervening early. This necessitates more teachers, and teachers who specialize in underachieving students. This assessment/intervention practice is continued from K–12.
- Pairing high–achieving schools with lower–income schools. These high–achieving schools can help with curriculum, instructional strategies, and management systems.
- Funding a program that pairs college/university students with low–performing K–12 students, to assist with homework, tutor, and help parents interact with the school system and in their children's education.
- Assigning more teachers to schools with higher concentrations of low performers.
- Increasing teacher pay, to attract more qualified applicants and to increase competition.

The above list presents only a few strategies that other countries with effective K–12 education systems use, and this doesn't mean we should rush to implement any or all of these strategies. However, if they've already been studied and found viable, the US should consider changing its policies and practices to reflect those of successful nations' education systems, provided that any change can be integrated into our schools' culture.

If improving our educational system is important to

us, we need to begin making changes beyond legislation, the emphasis on testing and teaching toward the test, mandating where and what schools children attend, and a carte blanch menu of optional activities/classes in lieu of rigor and relevant curriculum.

After decades of living with the same stagnant student achievement, is it time for change?

States, their communities, parents, school districts, education administrators, and teachers, will need to decide their educational priorities. Is ensuring each child receives the opportunity to attend a quality school a priority? Is our children's academic, physical, and social growth more important than elective classes, extracurriculars, and "open campus" all occurring during the school day? Can we continue to have it all? Can we better balance students' academic performance with their need for social and physical growth?

A school day only has so many hours, and the school year so many days. Globally, the US ranks in the middle in number of school days and hours. If we continue to use this schedule, it's imperative to effectively use this precious time.

I'm optimistic about our students' potential, and always have been. I can only hope educational reforms will occur in the near future and unleash our children's aptitude to learn.

I've observed the bureaucracy and barriers that impede administrators and teachers in our schools. The sad thing is that our children, with all their potential, become the victims. Every law, policy, and teachable moment should be considered according to what's in the students' best interests.

We need to review our students' growth, from K–12. We need to teach and care for each of them, challenge and guide them, and hold them accountable until they succeed—until they truly learn. We can do this by ensuring each student meets grade-level standards before passing them to the next grade. A great number of students across America aren't ready mentally/socially for promotion. Regardless, most students are passed on.

The public-school system will argue that they don't have the budget, available teachers, and support of parents to hold students back and repeat a necessary grade. It's likely this is as much a long-term challenge and commitment for parents as for the student themselves. If we're sincerely interested in our children's educations, it makes no sense and doesn't aid students to place them in the next grade without the possibility for success. We're setting them up for failure, and that's precisely what most do. In reality, students who repeat a grade level obtain an extra year of free public education and preparation for adulthood.

Our youth participate in a public-school system with short school days, often inconsistent curriculum rigor and relevancy, and a prevalent societal acceptance of the more "well-rounded" student. Many of our children follow this path, although not all students and their families. Parents who are involved and take an active interest in their child's education overcome this reality, and their student benefits.

We also need an improved system to assess teacher performance. Teacher tenure should be based more on performance than on years of service. Additionally, states need to conduct objective, transparent reviews of teachers' unions and their benefit to students, teachers, and the community.

It will take the people's will to make necessary policy changes without relying on the federal government. And little change will occur without parents' support.

Also, our priorities differ depending on students' needs and circumstances. We have many English learners, special needs, and "at-risk" students in public schools. Many of these students have numerous challenges and factors that impact their ability to learn and succeed.

Our educational policy is and should always remain teaching and using all resources to address each child's needs.

Our country doesn't benefit from more laws or slogans to raise our children's academic achievement. What we need is a team effort from state officials, educational administrators, school boards, parents, school staffs, and teachers to ensure all students succeed. "No Child Left Behind" ... let's try again, this time ensuring we're committed to all children's learning.

We've examined a few social topics, including healthcare, law enforcement, immigration, and K–12 education. Further discussion could include current "hot topics," such as abortion, gay marriage, gun control, and infinite other topics. On many of these issues, recent surveys indicate that Americans are split 50/50 or 60/40, similar to our national voting results.

Living in a culturally diverse country has tremendous advantages and benefits. However, as we've become more diverse over time, our country's division has widened. In a democratic nation, each group's needs and desires challenges others. This can result, as we're seeing today, in few issues being agreed upon and implemented. Compounding this reality are group stubbornness and resistance to consider others' voices and needs. Thus sight is lost, as well as what may be in our country's best interests.

Justice Powell's statement regarding equal justice, and the above examples, lead us to believe we're drifting, and at times justice isn't applied equitably. In 2017, alone we observed numerous politicians at many levels abuse their power and few held accountable. The irony is most American's know this unequal and "unfair" justice lives, yet, there is no way to stop it.

In professional sports alone, there's been an increase of drug offenses, DUIs, domestic abuse, weapon violations, etc., yet the players play on, with little or no correction. Some owners have recently commented, "Everyone deserves a second chance." If so, why don't we all get a second chance and "play on"? This is just one example of special treatment for "special" people. And it may one reason NFL TV ratings have plummeted in 2017.

The disturbing reality of this unequal justice is that it separates our society, and we're becoming immune to the point of acceptance. Also, unequal justice sends a clear message to our youth: if you join one of these classes of people, you're privileged and will receive special treatment. If our children believe this, the cycle will continue.

How did we get here, and why has this inequality been permitted to continue? Have we become so permissive and lackadaisical that our nation's leaders rationalize this behavior in the best interests of all of us? Regardless of the excuses and rationale, it's not justice and it's not fair!

We need change. Many Americans have this view and voted in hopes of disrupting the status quo they find unacceptable. They desire a new life with honesty, vigor, and transparency. They want politicians who will infuse ethics in their politics and do the right thing, regardless of party affiliation. They want leadership—i.e., leaders who consider service to their constituents and country more important than their own egos and tenure. And they want people who are honest and willing to work with others and get things done.

What continues to unite us in a divided America, is our desire for integrity and morality in our government. It is important individuals continue identifying the values they and their communities hold. The vast majority of Americans want an Ethical moral society. Therefore, we must continue to expect and demand it and search for leaders with these qualities.

According to a *New York Post* article, "70 percent of Americans believe the country is divided as badly today as it was during the Vietnam era. ... Some 80 percent of those polled had little use for the House and Senate, [and] only 12 percent believe senators and representatives base their votes on 'core values' while 87 percent think they 'do whatever is needed to win reelection.' The poll showed 'limited trust' in other institutions, including the press."[53]

In such a divided America today, only change will reunite us. Here are a few thoughts, which don't necessarily present a recipe for success.

We have a red–and–blue colored country. And, no, it is not a result of one person or a group of people. This isn't a new phenomenon but has been growing over decades. It's not all about politics. Americans have been self–segregating by lifestyle for some time. We are colored by the way we think, where and how we live, and how we vote. Occasionally states change colors, but not often.

No one can tell another how or what to think, where and how to live, or how to vote. We hold these rights and freedoms sacred. There may be solutions to breaking the

53 *http://nypost.com//internet/news/hhechtman/America is most divided since Vietnam War: poll/10282017*

stubborn tug of war encumbering our society, and it begins with leadership.

I don't know about you, but I think we should get rid of the sorrowful red and blue and create something new and more descriptive of "we the people." Two colors don't describe American people or our states, and red is a dismal color for optimism.

Our states and their leaders have responsibilities and can influence growth. States cannot rely on the president, Congress, and federal funding for their futures. Each state should have—and it's assumed they do—short- and long-term plans to continuously improve their status, show growth, and maintain their citizens' welfare.

It's each state's responsibility to attract people, businesses, and tourists. It's their responsibility to be fiscally competent, provide safety and security, foster employment and educational opportunities, and so forth. Therefore, states must adapt to diverse lifestyles and their population's needs and desires.

Many people research the best states, cities, and towns to live in or visit, by examining different criteria. We look at employment opportunities, crime rates, education programs and schools, availability of hospitals, recreational availability, cost of living, housing costs, big city/small town, urban/rural living, etc. We all have quality of life needs and wants. Therefore, if states and cities want to attract more businesses, residents, and visitors, they need to provide quality services and products. If not, no change occurs. Progress can only occur with change.

In a *Time* article, "These States are the Happiest and Healthiest," more than 177,000 Americans were asked fifty-five questions in a 2016 Gallup survey. The answers were used to determine respondents' physical, emotional, financial, community and social well- being. The following ten states were ranked as having the highest well-being: Hawaii, Alaska, South Dakota, Maine, Colorado, Vermont, Arizona, Montana, Minnesota, and Texas.[54]

When many of us read these surveys, we're often skeptical, disagree, or want more information. If our state isn't included, we think the study must be flawed.

When you look at the criteria, do you see a trend among these top ten states? I do. However, to be fair, these surveys always contain a few surprises. But how I would like to have a beach house in Hawaii!

We as citizens can make a difference, if we choose to do so—for American justice to continue flourishing.

We need to listen to each other, be truthful, and consider others views with open minds considering compromise, when possible.

We as citizens need to be knowledgeable about our causes. We don't have to be experts, but need to understand the issues we're discussing.

---

54 *http://time.com//internet/articles/davidjohnson/These States Are the Happiest and Healthiest/02012017*

We as citizens need to accept constructive criticism and continue as energetic "team players" when our ideas aren't accepted.

We as citizens need to consider the best interests of the majority, even though that may conflict with our opinions and interests.

We as citizens need to be informed and vote, and consider the best-qualified, morally responsible candidate, even though it may not be our party's candidate.

We as citizens need to obey all laws, and treat others fairly, without prejudice or discrimination, and not demonstrate abuse of any kind.

There's an old saying, "do not discuss politics and religion." I have for a long time agreed with this advice. I've changed my mind. Obviously, one should consider the audience and environment they are in before doing. Many better opportunities than others...common sense prevails. Though, if each of us could meet the citizens needs list above there would be no need for this advice. People would listen and talk to each other again regardless of their differences.

States and cities providing the most important lifestyle needs of our generation are attracting and keeping the most people. Progressive, affordable, safe, and clean locations are where people want to live. Politics rarely come into play. However, justice or lack of it is a well-known and a critical must-have.

Just recently, Missouri passed Senate Bill 43, which raises the legal burden needed to sue businesses for discrimination based on race, religion, or gender.

The Missouri NAACP opposed the bill and decided to issue a travel advisory, warning visitors that their civil rights could be violated if they enter the state. This advisory is the first of its kind against one of our own states.[55]

Without significant background and study regarding this issue, one must wonder if there was a more reasonable approach to the state's judicial system and legislative decision than to affect all Missouri residents and the entire state. This kind of action certainly doesn't benefit the people of Missouri, and the connotation is that this state is discriminatory, and its people are prejudiced. Of course, this is untrue, though many may begin to believe otherwise.

It's no wonder we have hardline red and blue. Can you imagine how the good citizens of Missouri feel? And what is the next state we should avoid travel to?

Is the above citizens' needs to-do list realistic? Probably, although millions of Americans, in the red and blue states alike, accomplish few of these. They aren't high expectations, they're nothing new, and no one is going to be rewarded for doing them. It's basic citizenship that Americans should be pursuing. Do we all? Of course not, and for those who don't, there's no recourse but to leave them behind. They're a drag on American progress. Those

55 http://www.senate.mo.gov/17info/pdf-bill/intro/SB43.pdf

who care and make an effort inspire justice.

I often told my students, "Neither you nor I have had much to do with the establishment of our great nation. We should feel fortunate to be living in America, but it's also natural to take good things for granted. Appreciate what you have, and don't be envious of others—you never know until you wear their shoes." And I reminded them, "What you do in your lifetimes will make a difference to our nation's future."

As far as our nation's justice is concerned, we began with majestic principles and ideals, like no other nation before us, and over two centuries have developed astonishing rights and freedoms for many Americans. Along the way we have also stumbled, as prejudice and discrimination continue in our culture. We have separated into a red-and-blue society and, too often, elitist needs and wants become more important than those of the commoner.

Our politics and judicial practice must remain separate, without wavering. And when things go awry, we must revert to our Constitution, enforce its laws equitably, and use our judicial branch appropriately. No group or individual is above the law.

The reality is, we live in a just America, though with many imperfections. Goodness is beautiful and heartfelt; evil is heartbreaking and sorrowful. When justice is consistent and equitable, we have fairness. When it isn't, our hands go up, and we shout out, "It's not fair."

"It's Not Fair": How Can We Deal with Social Challenges in Today's Culture?

A few lines from a Poem, titled "Teardrop" Copyright @ Doug Vinson, Dec. 26, 2016

"I ask you to mind our earth, heed our existence upon it, care for our lives and all that will occur if we cannot consider beyond ourselves, if we are guided by uncertainty, when we fear the unknown, when we shun those who differ from us in skin color, in sex, in persuasion, if we turn or eyes away, ...when we mistake violence for the solution, when we won't bother to look past the wheelchair and to whom he really is, ... when women must lie in fear, when we steal identities, when evil hides, in anonymity, when we rest in apathy, indifferent to the pain of others, ... when we deny justice to one lonely voice, our world falls, stretching itself into a teardrop."

CHAPTER THREE

Not Supposed to be, Why me God?

My favorite topic in this theme of justice is a personal one, but common to us all at one time or other.

My younger sister died a few years ago, at a young age, much too soon. She burned in her small apartment one cold, wintery, Wisconsin evening, with no one there to help her. A witness ran out of the burning apartment in time to see her, on fire, trying to escape and jump from the second story into the snow. She couldn't muster the strength and agility to climb over the railing. She had no chance.

She'd been sick for many years, had multiple surgeries, and required numerous medications. Yet she loved her two sons, was playful, full of spunk, and always ready to challenge the world's conflicts, debating with me regularly.

She had lived a difficult life. She'd received few breaks. It was sad to watch. We could do little but love her.

At her service I asked God, "Why her? Why did she have to live a life of so much pain and unhappiness all the way to her death? Why her mother, sitting next to me? And why me, God?" Then I felt confused and bewildered, wondering why I was concerned about myself. Shame on me!

Many have cried, "Why me, God? And why did you let this happen?" because something sorrowful and senseless has occurred. You quickly feel God has let you down, or is punishing you or someone else. "It's not fair." A multitude of thoughts enter our minds when experiencing pain and sorrow. Our thoughts, believe it or not, are normal and common.

According to Timothy Keller, in a CNN article "My Faith: The Danger of Asking God 'Why Me?" a few answers come to mind. The first possible answer is, "'I guess this proves there is no God." The problem with this thinking is that the problem of senseless suffering does not go away if you abandon belief in God."

"The second response to suffering is: 'While there is a God, he's not completely in control of everything. He couldn't stop this." "But that kind of God, doesn't really fit our definition of 'God.' So that thinking hardly helps us with reconciling God and suffering." In this thinking, we kind of believe, but we kind of don't.

"The third answer to the worst kind of suffering—

seemingly senseless death—is: 'God saves some people and lets others die because he favors and rewards good people.' The Bible forcefully rejects the idea that people who suffer more are worse people than those who are spared suffering."

"The fourth answer to suffering is in the face of an all-powerful God is that God knows what he's doing, so be quiet and trust him." But Keller describes this response as "cold" and declares that "the Bible gives us much more with which to face the terrors of life."

"God did not create a world with death and evil in it. It is the result of humankind turning away from him. We were put into this world to live wholly for him, and when instead we began to live for ourselves everything in our created reality began to fall apart, physically, socially, and spiritually. Everything became subject to decay."

"But God did not abandon us. Only Christianity of all the world's major religions teaches that God came to Earth in Jesus Christ and became subject to suffering and death himself, dying on the cross to take the punishment our sins deserved, so that someday he can return to Earth to end all suffering without ending us."

Keller continues, "We don't know the reason God allows evil and suffering to continue, or why it is so random, but now at least we know what the reason isn't, what it can't be."[56]

---

56 http://religion.blogs.CNN.com/2012/08/My Faith: The danger of asking God, "why me?"

We do know that he loves and cares for us. He gives us life and opportunity and wants each of us to live a good life. Our course of action is left entirely up to us. No one is exempt from life's trials and perils. Where we differ is that some are better prepared than others to cope with and withstand life's many challenges.

Remember, you're not alone. All of us experience grief and suffering, and we immediately look to God for meaning and pray for his help. Too often, what we expect God to say or do for us doesn't instantly occur, and we feel let down. We feel betrayed, since we have done good, followed him, believed in him, and shared his love. So why me, God?

God's goodness and mercy is what we believe and know is true. It is our faith that, every minute of every day, through ups and downs, keeps us going. He is in each one of us and won't give up on us. Therefore, with everlasting belief, we must turn to our faith to guide us through life's many challenges. After all, life is a short and unpredictable journey.

It was far too short for a previous student of mine who passed away recently in her twenties. She was an outstanding high school student, bright, caring, happy, and a servant for others. She graduated college cum laude, and became a police officer. By all accounts, this officer was the very best in her training and on the job. She completed all her police tasks with excellence, and then would remain on the job to ensure all involved parties were treated with the utmost care and dignity. She was a perfectionist, loved people, and was always true to herself and others. She was admired by many for her sensitive and warm personality and genuine and loving smile. Just the way I remember her.

Her life ended to soon. It simply was not fair! Why oh why? It seems when we determine we have life figured out and begin to understand and adapt to tragedy, sorrow, and unfairness in our lives, we continually must relearn and renew. All too often there are no immediate answers or resolutions.

Each person who knew this young lady will grieve in their own way, in their own space and time. What we have in common is her fond memory and our faith, our hope, and our love. This human experience is life and it is hard!

Margaret Fishback Powers wrote the following essay you may want to remember and refer to, titled "Footprints":

> "One night I dreamed a dream. I was walking along a beach with my Lord. Across the dark sky flashed scenes from my life. For each scene, I noticed two sets of footprints in the sand, one belonging to me and one to my Lord.

> "When the last scene of my life shot before me I looked back at the footprints in the sand. There was only one set of footprints. I realized that this was at the lowest and saddest times of my life. This really bothered me and I questioned the Lord about my dilemma.

"'Lord, You told me when I decided to follow You, You would walk and talk with me all the way. But I'm aware that during the most troublesome times of my life there is only one set of footprints. I just don't understand why, when I need You most, You would leave me.'

"He whispered, 'My precious child, I love you and will never leave you, never, ever during your trials and testings. When you saw only one set of footprints, it was then that I carried you."[57]

During tough times, it's difficult to believe, yet it's this belief that gives us the courage to continue another day. Rather than asking God to perform a miracle or show himself as he did with doubting Thomas, we look to family, friends, community, and clergy for comfort and prayer. God is with us during these trying times. His footprints may not be visible, but he's carrying us via others' love and solace. We need each other.

Who more so than today's youth are polarized by social media? As if life isn't challenging enough in childhood and adolescence, they're susceptible to abuse, bullying, self-destruction, and worse. Some are better prepared in life, socially and emotionally, and can avoid and/or overcome this potential negativity. Far too many cannot. When something important to them doesn't turn out the way they want, and it becomes social news, they have difficulty coping. They often feel angry, punished, and alone. It may be as simple

57 http://www.wowzone.com/footprints.html

as a relationship problem or something much more serious. Regardless, they need friends in their lives, peers they trust and who care about them. To youth, friendship is extremely important—I've seen it time and time again.

Even people who are best equipped and prepared for sorrow will experience different stages of grief. We all feel sorrow and pain in our own unique way. People may not experience all stages of grief, or they may have many. There is no recipe for what and how to feel in a certain timeframe. It would be so nice if there were.

In the book *On Grief and Grieving*, coauthored by Elisabeth Kübler-Ross and David Kessler, five common stages are presented that make up our learning to live with grief and despair.

The first is denial. "In this stage, the world becomes meaningless and overwhelming. Shock and denial occur. We are not sure we can go on. Denial is a needed emotion to survive loss. Denial and shock help us make survival possible. There is hope in denial. It is a natural process of letting in only as much as we can handle. We become stronger during this stage as our denial begins to fade."

The second is *anger*, "also a necessary stage of the healing process." The truth is that anger has no limits. It can extend to anyone or everyone you encounter, including God." This is where you may question God repeatedly.

"Anger is strength, and is necessary to combat our grief. Anger is normal, part of being human, and we should not fear this emotion it is just another indication of the intensity of our love."

Stage three is *bargaining*. "We want life returned to what it was. Guilt is often bargaining's companion. The 'if onlys' cause us to find fault with ourselves and what we 'think' we could have done differently. We remain in the past, struggling with the pain."

The fourth stage is *depression*. "After bargaining, our attention moves squarely to the present. Empty feelings present themselves, and grief enters our lives. This depressive state feels as though it will last forever. It hurts, and the hurt lingers for some time. This is not mental illness, but a natural and appropriate response to a great loss. Depression is one of the many necessary steps along the way."

And the fifth and final stage is *acceptance*. "This stage is about accepting the reality of our loss, and it is permanent. We don't like this, but eventually we accept it. We learn to live with it. We can never replace what has been lost, but we make new relationships and move on. We begin to live again, only after giving grief its time."[58]

In the acceptance phase, we clearly see why family and friends are so important to our healing process. This time is often difficult and can be softened with others' support and compassion. We need each other.

---

58 *http"//grief.com//internet/article/Amessage from David Kessler/The 5 Stages of Grief*

My students often discussed friendship and relationships, including their criteria for real friendship. Interestingly, they were in accord as to what friendship meant to them. We discussed how one person may have 350 "friends" on social media, but only have a handful of sincere and caring friends. And how a person with a few good friends may be just as popular as the person who believes everyone is their friend.

In a time of need, people quickly determine who their real friends are, the ones who will be there for them.

Faith, hope and love, as I learned with repetition after repetition in school. It's as if the good sisters had no other materials for lessons. How I wish I had those days to live over, and what would I have learned. Unfortunately, as an altar boy, I was more interested in which pastor would be serving mass before school, to determine my wine consumption opportunities after the service. The red wine was delicious.

Faith, hope, and love. These three virtues exist when we need them and even when we don't. All we have to do is believe.

Too often, natural disasters, accidents, disease, cruelty, and abuse take life from us or sap us of our spirit and confidence to look forward to another day. Millions of undeserving people are affected yearly. Why were they chosen? Why at such an early age? What did they do to deserve such an unfair destiny? Seems we are always asking these questions.

Slavery, the Holocaust, the atomic bomb, terrorism at home and abroad, biological and chemical weapon use, hurricanes and earthquakes, homicides and sexual assaults, and mental and physical disease are examples of how life can be shortened.

Since the attack on our nation on September 11, 2001, I made a pledge to myself to speak every year on that day. I've spoken at high schools and in communities each year since. My thought was that it would be good to heal each year, reflect, and remember. The first few years my words mainly focused on the facts, actions of the perpetrators, the 3,000 or so victims, and hope for the future.

As time went on, I realized that many in my audience weren't in school or even born during this horrific tragedy. How could I convey what occurred that day—why thousands died without cause, who the brave souls were on the ground and in the air, how many people were lost, how to make sense of it all. Why God, did it happen at all, and why did so many innocent people have to die so tragically? It wasn't fair.

What was most amazing each September 11th morning were the students themselves. Each year we had a 45-minute ceremony for all 3,500 students, as well as staff and community members. Two thousand or so students in the high-school quad, and the remaining students watching live on TV. The Junior Reserve Officers' Training

Corps (JROTC), school band and choir, Associated Student Body (ASB), video and audio staff, the school TV staff and students, and student color guard all come together to present the ceremony.

This annual ceremony at Vista Murrieta High School (VMHS), in Murrieta, California, has become a student-managed event. In 2015 the Air Force recognized it as the "best seen in the nation." It's no wonder: VMHS is an example of students buying into the culture of the school "CLASS," Character, Leadership, Attitude, Scholarship, and Service, with leadership, compassion, and exceptional attitude. The students have faith in the staff, their peers, and the community. They humbly progress with obvious hope for their futures and their friends. It's a wonderful teaching experience that no teacher wants to miss.

This year, 2017, marked the 16th anniversary of September 11, 2001. We remember our heroes, our togetherness, patriotism, the victims, and our sorrow. No group, politician, celebrity, person kneeling during the national anthem, or anyone else could take this spirit away from us. American flags streaming down neighborhood streets, positive voices spoke, with people united in prayer. We remember as flags across America are lowered, and we take time to come together again.

As we reflect and renew, we're more separated as a nation than 16 years ago. Our faith and hope in one another and our nation has again been challenged. What kind of society do we want our children to grow up in? Is living with diversity itself rationalization for our indifference and separation? Is it still important for each American to have respect and love for our country, or is this value no longer important? Hopefully, each of us continues to have faith and hope.

My first words on 9/11 to Murrieta, California, high-school students, and later in the day to the Temecula, California, community (words slightly changed for the community). These words and thoughts have evolved over the years.

Good morning.

Today let us remember, reflect, and renew together and dedicate the next few minutes to the men, women, and children who lost their lives; those brave people who gave their lives; and the heroes who responded on September 11, 2001. We will never forget them, nor the last time we saw them, as they prepared for their journey, waved goodbye, and left us forever.

Emma was a 6-year-old first grader who watched the fires on top of the Twin Towers and the terrified people trapped in the floors waving desperately at her on the ground. She then watched them smashing windows and leaping out. Her father rushed her into their apartment. Months later Emma had nightmares of people just sort of floating off and landing and running away. Her father let her believe that's what happened. His comment was, "It's hard to make sense of something for a kid that you cannot make sense of yourself."

September 11, 2001, will be remembered and hopefully never forgotten as one of the most horrific events experienced in our United 50 States. Nineteen men trained and educated in the US were armed to take us down. This attack on our country certainly continues to affect every American, and likely every person in the world in some way.

It should have been a perfect day. The skies were clear, blue, and beautiful, with miles and miles of visibility across the Northeast and at home here in Southern California. But what should have been was not. The day's beauty would become ugly, and all the blue would fade to a murky fog of hatred, fear, and terror.

On the East Coast, people had started work, on the West Coast; we were awaking or making our way. And then we heard it, saw it, felt it, as if it were upon each of us, our families, and our loved ones.

We will remember this day much like our preceding generation remembers what they were doing on Pearl Harbor Day.

We will always remember the towers raining debris on Lower Manhattan and hundreds of brave firemen and policemen who were caught in the storm and killed in the collapse.

We will remember the thousands of New Yorkers who ran through the streets in terror, ashes and smoke-filled grounds, as onlookers gasped, helpless and horrified.

We will remember the sunny day that went dark. By the afternoon of September 11, 2001, black and gray had blanketed Manhattan. Our nation was crippled and in pain.

Over 3,000 dead, at the World Trade Center, the Pentagon, and in the air. Men, women, children, Americans, and non-Americans—it made no difference. It was injustice at its worst!

Remember:

Dorothy deAraujo, 80, Long Beach, California;

Sanae Mori, 27, Tokyo, Japan;

Pedro Checo, 35, New York, New York;

Zoe Falkenberg, 8, and her sister Dana, 3, University Park, Maryland.

Remember.

Why ... Why did Dana have to die? For months

all of us, like Emma and her father, tried to understand the unthinkable, the unbelievable.

Today, as we continue to reflect and still feel the pain, anger, grief, vulnerability, and anxiety of what lies in the future, we Americans remain steadfast and tenacious in our love of country and willingness to serve whenever and wherever needed. That's the MOTTO we have adopted here with CLASS—living your lives—assisting and motivating others, being positive contributors to your school and community, and just smiling and caring for one another.

It often takes enormous courage to show compassion and hug someone in need and tell them how much you care and how important they are. Truly, what is more important in life than how we treat one another? Will you be ready to serve and contribute to your country? Are you this kind of person?

Many of you are already placing others before yourselves and taking on the most rigorous challenges. Savor each challenge, solve it, and then accept another! In the years ahead our country will need you. Will you be ready?

As you grow to adulthood, remember to take a few moments, now and then, to reflect and develop an understandable connection to what happened on September 11, 2001.

All Americans will continue to be challenged daily, depending on the times. If history serves us well, we will remain strong together and continue to overcome our most rigorous challenges.

Charles Dickens had it right in "A Tale of Two Cities" with the insight, "It was the best of times, it was the worst of times."

September 11, 2001, was certainly the worst of times. But it did not cause Americans to fear or lose their cool. Quite the opposite. We are adapting to living with terrorism, even as we continue the struggle to defeat it. We reflect, adapt, and renew. As we always have.

During these difficult times, and there will be more challenges in our lives, always keep your HOPE—for yourself, your family and friends, and your country.

On September 11th, much of America remembers those we lost. Let's also remember today those, like Emma, who cannot forget, and Dana, who was never given the chance to remember or forget.

Thank you, and stay strong today!

In remembrance of September 11, I was surprised at one of our church services. We sang all four verses of "America the Beautiful." In church, in today's climate, I pondered: I don't remember ever getting past the first verse.

The third verse says:

O beautiful for heroes proved in liberating strife,

Who more than self their country loved

And mercy more than life!

America! America!

May God thy gold refine,

Till all success be nobleness,

And every gain divine!

Is our society becoming callous to personal tragedy, and others pain and sorrow? In the cases of terrorism and homicides alone—Oklahoma City, New York City, Boston, San Bernardino, Las Vegas, Orlando, Chicago and other cities—the daily news is so overwhelming, that we commonly hear conversations like the following:

"Did you hear about the explosion today in city X?"

"Yes, that's terrible. What time are you going to lunch?"

Have victims' faces, their names, and their families become a blur, almost irrelevant?

You're right to think, well, what can I do about it? What is expected of me? How can I make a difference?

Take a moment to reflect and say a prayer for those in pain and sorrow, and when possible provide your

compassion and faith toward a better tomorrow. Our love,
friendship, and faith, coupled with time itself, can help the
healing process.

Isaiah 6:86 says, "And I heard the voice of the Lord
saying: 'Whom shall I send, and who will go for us?' Then I
said: 'Here am I; send me.'"

So when times are difficult, we know God is with us,
and therefore we don't need to question his love. We must
always have faith—confident trust or belief in God.

And we must love, which scripture calls "the greatest
of these," (1 Corinthians 13:13), is described in the Bible
as being self-sacrificial rather than self- seeking. It seeks
what is best for others rather than self and is based on God,
who is love (1 John 4:8). True love is appropriately defined
in one of the Bible's most famous passages, John 3:16:
"For God so loved the world, as to give his only begotten
Son; that whosoever believeth in him, may not perish, but
may have life everlasting."

No matter how ready and prepared we are to meet grief
and sorrow, we need to feel free to express our feelings,
and not fear our emotions and grief. Who would we be
without them? And we need others, who care for us during
trying times.

CHAPTER FOUR

You Control Your Success and Happiness

My mother often told me, "always live your life with balance and moderation, and avoid extremism." She told me this applied to everything: politics, school, work, recreation, food and drink, etc. By balancing my life, she would say, I would have more opportunities to find my own success and ultimate happiness. How wise and true this is. Her reason for this lighthearted lesson was my spending too much time on athletics, and avoiding responsibilities and missing other opportunities. But she loved watching my baseball games.

It's a lesson I carried with me in life, and fortunately applied at a young age. We do have control of our lives and have so many opportunities, if we don't take ourselves and others too seriously and live a balanced life.

We should always strive to be good citizens and have an awareness of the world around us. We should question justice and fairness in our society, think for ourselves, and serve and show compassion for those who need us. And there must be time in our lives to balance the questions of justice and fairness, and concentrate on our own happiness.

At the end of the 2017 school year, a few National Honor students and the advisor to the National Honor Society at our school asked me if I would provide a TED Talk to the students. I immediately said yes, and asked what they would like me to talk about. They replied, "Anything you want." I then asked how long should I speak, and the reply was, "For as long as you like." It's a good thing I didn't ask how I should dress.

My first thought as a soon-to-be-retired teacher, and one who talks to himself, was, "I finally get to talk about the Green Bay Packers—their history, how the Wisconsin residents have ownership, and a current overview and prediction for the 2017 season. Oh, what fun!" Then reality hit me: administrators, adults, and 50 or so of the smartest students in school would be there. I must remain professional to the end, I reminded myself. My original idea was ridiculous!

I then decided on a topic, taking control of success and happiness in our lives. One thing I knew is that this topic is relevant to them.

Aware that my audience would be overachievers, I had to be careful not to underestimate their knowledge, but at the same time present a practical and realistic approach to life, through my eyes.

They were wonderful. Their eyes seemed interested, they smiled and even laughed. They applauded at the end. That's what National Honor Society students do, I told myself. What did they really think? I'll never know.

The following are a few of my thoughts to the students.

We convened in our beautiful school theater, dimly lit, comfortable and clean. I always felt fortunate to use this theater. How could anyone, adult or student, not be successful here, I thought?

I began by asking the students to close their eyes and consider this question: if they had one wish for what success would be in their life, what would it be? After a few minutes, there was a lot of communication between students, as they shared their thoughts. They quickly found they had many commonalities/similarities and differences. But due to time restrictions, all the students couldn't share their responses.

In life, all too often we're told how to become a leader, how to behave, how to become successful, how to do this and that. We're informed of success quotes—"The ten secrets of success, the must-have qualities of leadership, follow these steps towards real happiness" etc.—the laundry list that teachers, parents, coaches, ministers, motivational speakers, and most adults communicate and preach to youth. One generation after another. All in good faith and hope, I believe! Unfortunately, in many cases, it goes in one ear and out the other.

Recently, I heard a speech about success. In my opinion, it was well written and presented; however, I remembered little, didn't absorb the main points, and therefore was unable to reflect on or use the information. It was relevant, but it didn't stick. My point is that there's no magical "to-do list" to guarantee a successful and happy life.

No matter how old one is, where they're from or what they do for a living, we all share the desire to be successful. Each person's definition of success is different; there are as infinite opinions and wishes as stars in the sky! Because we're all unique, there are no obvious "right" answers. The dictionary defines success as the accomplishment of one's goal, the desired result of an attempt, or one that succeeds. That is kind of stale, let's break it down some.

Success is comparing with our own *best self*. It's a journey, not a destination. Successful people steadily move toward worthwhile, predetermined personal and professional goals throughout their lifetimes ... a pursuit during their entire lifetimes! It's about how badly you want something and how hard you're willing to work for it. In other words, tenacity—it's about the traits you possess to help you get there.

Each of our goals can have a vast range, from striving for a loving family, happiness, and good friends, to achieving personal benchmarks, career status, recognition, admiration, a sense of importance, or to being a servant to others, or a combination of these.

We all want to become successful and happy, and have life stay that way. When we begin to see the common factors that influence eventual success, one's *character* stands out. More than anything else, success depends on the ability to keep striving forward, with ours heads up. We must be determined and persistent in the face of disappointment and occasional failure.

Coach John Wooden, who had 27-year career with UCLA men's basketball, summed up how patience and faith helps us achieve success: Patience, like faith, requires work. In his book, *The Essential Wooden*, he writes, "it is calm self-possession in confronting the necessary fits and starts, obstacles and delays that are part and parcel of achieving anything worthwhile."[59]

When we truly reach success, then we can pursue our passions, and the greatest of these is *serving* others. Character is to success as service is to happiness.

Often I would ask my students, what was the better feeling at holiday time—receiving gifts or giving them? Almost unanimously, the students said giving was more special to them. I would ask them rhetorically, have you

59 *"The Essential Wooden: A Lifetime of Lessons on Leaders and Leadership,"* January 5, 2007, by John Wooden and Steve Jamison

ever seen someone unhappy while serving someone else in need? The room went silent. A good sign—the students were thinking.

For centuries, many have agreed that happiness is found in serving others.

Years ago, it was challenging getting students to serve. Those days have come and gone. Now we have so many students volunteering in our school programs alone, that we often must have a cut off. Sure, you get your required service hours, but many, like you, don't even document all your service. You do it because you have a passion to help others regardless who they are and where they came from. It's pleasurable, and you feel happy. These feelings keep you coming back, doing more. I know this, I have seen you!

We're happiest serving when we're doing something we enjoy. Working with children, tutoring your peers, assisting the elderly, cleaning the environment, helping the homeless, and the list goes on. Happy people are often those who are helping others. Never feel pressured to serve. Do it when you feel generous, compassionate, and a have sense of purpose. Do it when you wish. Finding your niche may be your lifelong service.

I read a wonderful book recently, entitled *The Happiness Advantage: The Seven Principles of Positive Psychology That Fuel Success and Performance at Work*, by Shawn Achor. In the book he describes how our happiness increases our productivity, and many simple little things in our lives can make us much happier. It's a practical, easy read, and I highly recommend it.

Serving and caring for others is one thing that makes us feel good. Without a doubt, we have many opportunities to care for and serve others. When you wonder if you're making a difference and have purpose in life, ask yourself questions like, "Am I placing others above myself? Have I made another person's day better? Have I contributed or volunteered? Have I exceeded my fair share?" We can serve in our school, in the workforce, in the community—anywhere and everywhere.

Recently, I received a recommendation form to be completed on behalf of one of my prior students. She's applying to become a volunteer assistant position for the terminally ill at a major medical facility. I thought to myself, "Good for her; she will excel," and completed the recommendation.

The key is to sustain our passion throughout a lifetime of service. The more we enjoy serving others, the more purpose and happiness we'll have in our lives.

Every year I teach, while discussing equality and citizenship, I would hold out both hands with my palms up. In one was baby Y in the other baby X, born on the same date, of different colors and cultures. My question was, do these two babies, at birth, have the same opportunities in life? What do you think? (Paused)

The students discussed in groups, and then we

discussed as an entire class. The responses ranged from yes, no, not sure, to yes—but the babies may have different opportunities. One of my favorite experiences teaching was when I observed students working together, critically thinking. This small exercise was no exception. And of course, after the discussion, the students often asked how I felt. Normally, I don't respond. But for this exercise, I shared.

In these first days of their lives, neither baby is destined to be more successful with more opportunities than the other. For example, baby Y has no greater opportunity to become a leader, or more successful than baby X. The babies are born equal but may have different opportunities; in this I agree with the students. Therefore, what occurs throughout a person's life determines their opportunities. It's like students beginning the school year on equal footing with a perfect 4.0 GPA, and then the work they do, decisions they make, and attitude they possess influence their academic success.

Furthermore, in assuming equality at birth, and similar or different opportunities, no one should say they were born without any opportunity, and that there is no justice—thus, "It's not fair." There's no excuse to quit, become angry, or blame others. Everyone is born with opportunity.

All people on earth have their unique personalities, talents, skills, potential, and opportunities in life. What's different is people's ethnicity, religious beliefs, social class, gender, age, education, family backgrounds, disabilities, and locations. These factors influence opportunity, and often result in unfair treatment.

Common examples of unfair treatment are experienced, older people being passed over for employment or promotion in favor of younger, less experienced and qualified employees. Or highly qualified people with disabilities eliminated from employment consideration, solely based on their special needs. The TV show *The Good Doctor* comes to mind: an autistic, young doctor who's very intelligent and qualified faces workplace discrimination and perseveres to save lives. Do you believe it is realistic? (Pause)

Obviously, certain people have more difficult challenges using their uniqueness during their lifetimes. It's not as easy as telling someone or a group of people, "Do this or that," or "Try harder—it's your responsibility," and be done with it.

When people experience repeated failure and have little support and guidance, they often quit, isolate themselves, become unproductive, rebel, or worse. Their perception of the people in their lives can become negative, and the world around them is "not fair." For many this reality wasn't derived at birth but by life itself.

Many people have come from difficult backgrounds, experienced the toughest obstacles, and have succeeded. How did they become successful, against all odds? I have

my opinions; you may have yours. Here are a few of my
favorite examples: (showed with visual aid)

- Jackie Robinson, the first African American to play
  in Major League Baseball in the modern era. (One of
  his quotes is, "A life is not important except for the
  impact it has on other lives.")
- Helen Keller, the first blind and deaf person to earn
  a college degree.
- Ludwig van Beethoven, who began losing his hearing
  at the age of 26, he continued to compose music,
  and the majority of his most-beloved works were
  composed when he was already deaf.
- Vincent Van Gogh, a famous artist, who was admitted
  to several insane asylums and hospitals during the
  course of his life.
- Albert Einstein, Nobel-Prize winning physicist, who
  had a learning disability and didn't speak until he was
  three years old. He also failed repeatedly in his life.
- Tom Cruise, famous actor, who grew up in near
  poverty with a father who beat him.
- Victor Frankl, who wrote *Man's Search for Meaning*,
  an extremely influential book in the US. He was
  imprisoned in several Nazi concentration camps,
  including Auschwitz. His wife and family were killed.
- Oprah Winfrey, an extremely influential and talented
  entertainer, best known for her multi-award-
  winning talk show *The Oprah Winfrey Show*. Born

into poverty, she was raped at age nine and became pregnant at 14; her son died in infancy.

- Nelson Mandela, who worked hard to train as a lawyer, despite South Africa's apartheid system. He played a critical role in bringing about the end of apartheid. He was awarded The Nobel Peace Prize.

- Mahatma Gandhi, for his nonviolent protests against the British domination of India, he was incarcerated several times. Through his work he helped create independent India in 1947.

- Jesse Owens, despite experiencing racial discrimination in his native US, he became a world hero and gold medalist at the 1936 Berlin Olympics.

- J. K. Rowling, who for many years struggled as a single mother living on benefits. After many of her writings were rejected, she published *Harry Potter and the Sorcerer's Stone*, one of the best-selling books of all time.

- Howard Schultz, born to poor Jewish parents, who was the first member of his family to attend college. Working his way up from a salesperson, he became CEO of Starbucks, earning him $1.6 billion dollars by 2013.

- Roberto Clemente, my favorite baseball player, was born in a poor family in Puerto Rico. He was a Puerto Rican professional baseball player who played 18 seasons in Major League Baseball (MLB) for the Pittsburgh Pirates, He was inducted into the

National Baseball Hall of Fame in 1973, becoming the first Latin American and Caribbean player to be enshrined. On December 31, 1972, he died in a plane crash while en route to deliver aid to earthquake victims in Nicaragua.

Many people have grown up in difficult circumstances and/or have had physical or mental disadvantages, and still they've succeeded. We can learn much from them. They inspire and motivate us. Interesting, these people rarely have spent time dwelling on the perceived "fairness" in their lives, but much time describing their many opportunities.

These people who have overcome obstacles to better themselves show little resentment or anger toward society. Many are contributing to or serving their communities with their actions. They understand the realities existing in our communities and homes; they have been there. We need these people, and they need us.

Nelson Mandela once wrote, "No one is born hating another person because of the color of his skin, or his background, or his religion. People must learn to hate, and if they can learn to hate, they can be taught to love, for love comes more naturally to the human heart than its opposite."[60]

Karin Tydén, in her article, "Do We All Have the Same Opportunities?" suggests that we do have similar opportunities: "For instance, we have the ability to change

---

60 http//goodreads.com//internet/articles/Mandela/quote

how we think. How much we can change our thoughts, maybe depends on our circumstances, but we can ALWAYS change something. We can always make the effort and make the best of what we have." She also "disagree[s] with people who place the responsibility on all others (community, parents, schools, politicians, etc.) to make my life better." She answers the question her article title poses, "Yes, no, sometimes."

Tydén concludes, "But an even more important question for me is: Do you make something out of the opportunities you have?"[61]

Over the years I've seen many people fail, despite growing up with all the advantages of money, a quality education, and good health. I've also observed others who have started off less advantaged, impaired and impeded by emotional and physical illness and poverty, and still managed to succeed. I've seen valedictorians receive college scholarships and later drop out or be disenrolled from college, and military officers who made poor decisions and received dishonorable discharges. There have been politicians who were impeached or forced to resign due to their actions and behavior.

Or, closer to home, the number of freshmen students each year who tell me they used to do this or that, but have quit. They used to be athletes, participate in drama, or play a musical instrument. At the "old" age of 14 years, they're

---

61 http://linkedin.com//internet/articles/Tyden/Do we all have the same opportunities?/08012015

done. When I asked them why, few could answer.

On their way to success? Hardly! They have for the time being, simply stopped growing, because they are afraid of failure and see themselves as inferior.

When people lose their self-esteem, they're incapable of conceiving their goals and have lost their confidence and drive. For various reasons, they've adopted a "kick me" habit, with negative feelings regarding their self-worth and worthiness of happiness and success. This lack of self-respect exists amongst children, adults, males, and females. Many of you have observed students with this inferiority complex, and possibly helped them. What they need is our empathy and friendship, not our sympathy and indulgence.

I am going to share a short and realistic story of a woman who had little self-esteem and confidence. With some help and counsel she turned her life around. For the first time in her life she began experiencing success and happiness.

Sarah's Story

Sarah, a spinster, was proud of her own little apartment. But she lived near her married brother, and somehow, she often found herself doing the housework over there while her childless sister-in-law attended an interior decorating course.

Her brother borrowed from Sarah's rainy-day fund and never got around to paying her back. Her sister-in-law insisted on redecorating Sarah's apartment; Sarah didn't like the results but accepted them. The sister – in – law's forced involvement with Sarah started over simple coffee together; however, the discussion grew and became worse.

Concurrently, Sarah was having troubles at her office. She was quiet, rarely smiled or spoke to cohorts. She was living with a "poor me," "old maid" personality. Soon after the apartment redecoration, a good friend heard Sarah's story and talked with her. The friend made it quite clear to Sarah that she was being used, and she was permitting this manipulation to occur. Furthermore, in order to facilitate change, she would need to take charge of her life. She asked Sarah, "What is it that you like?"

They spoke together regarding Sarah's need to confront her inner self, her self-respect and well-being. At first, Sarah resisted such counsel. However, soon a change occurred.

A few weeks later the sister-in-law was angry. Sarah had redecorated her apartment to suit herself. Why? Because that was what she liked.

Later, when Sarah's lease ended, she moved to the other end of town because she liked living there.

Over time, Sarah renewed her self-esteem and restored her dignity. It led to a change of office character, and she became a more relaxed and tolerant person. She dressed better, looked better, felt better. She asked her brother to start paying back what he owed her, in a confident, strong tone, and he did. And Sarah joined a hiking club and established many new friends. She now has many goals and spends more time than ever with others in a new life of happiness.

Sarah's challenge became a personal success. She clearly had the option to quit and remain a spinster in her dark world, alone and unhappy. The difference was that Sarah had received a friend's compassion and care, which ultimately provided her the strength and confidence to change. She took charge of her life.[62]

Many people will walk away from a challenge because they find it too hard, whereas successful people love challenges. These people realize easy things aren't worth the effort; they want the challenge. Their goal is to be the best always at whatever they do—that's their passion. They're optimistic people.

I've heard that fear is the most common emotion commanded against in the Bible: "Do not be afraid!" It makes sense. Whenever we grow, there is fear. Whenever we do something new and face change, there is fear. Whenever we push ourselves to new heights or expand beyond our comfort zones, there is fear. This is the nature of life.

I like success stories, and there are many. A friend I grew up with couldn't attend school because of a physical illness and later in life owned his own successful business after failing twice. Another friend with one arm played baseball with me throughout high school. A Hispanic student I taught

---

62 *"Take Charge of your Life", J.K. Summerhill, copyright 1968, pp. 29–30*

was an English learner. Her parents spoke Spanish only. She earned a near 4.0 GPA, received a $25,000 college scholarship, and later graduated college.

Many successful authors have gone through a prolonged period of rejection. Most of the finest athletes in the world have failed repeatedly. Many of our greatest presidents have failed in campaigns, including Grant, Lincoln, and Washington. They all overcame failure.

We must be able to emotionally absorb failure, but certainly not accept it. There is a great difference! Can we raise our children to be fearless of failure, and to support them when they do fail? We need to provide them with the confidence and emotional tools necessary to respond to failure with renewed passion for their goals.

Our actions and decisions define our success in life. Everything starts in our minds and ripples outward, so what happens around us reflects our own inner world. Me, myself, and I. In other words, we control more of our lives than most of us realize. This seems to be common sense, but do we always apply it in our lives?

The pursuit of success and happiness requires us to be physically and mentally healthy. We need to be physically healthy to have the energy to engage in life and pursue our goals, as well as continuously using our minds to learn and grow.

Continually learning is a key activity in a successful and purposeful life. Successful people are always learning. I remember being told by an adult, "When we quit learning, we die." Somewhat dramatic, but has stayed with me over the years.

We learn daily from other people, things happening around us, our experiences, and self-destruction. I hear students talk about how they look forward to not returning to school after graduation, as if their learning—reading, writing, communicating, and thinking—is over.

When people stop learning, they become stagnant. They've stopped moving forward, like murky river water. They've stopped tapping into their potential. We want to always be moving forward, and this requires using our minds. For these people, young and old, little do they know that their learning never stops. You are fortunate—you have learned this valuable lesson at early ages.

Our emotional balance and health is just as important. We want to feel good about ourselves, have a positive self-image. Believe in your ability to succeed! If one can't function emotionally, success is impossible.

Likewise, we all need positive relationships in our lives—people who love and support us. The people we choose in life reflect our very selves. These relationships will follow you a lifetime. You determine your relationships.

Yes, a life together. We're much better off in life connected to others. To allow others to know us, and to let down our guard, is healthy growth. It is saying to ourselves, "I want to change, work on myself, and become a stronger and better person." We need this connection and sense of community in our lives; it stimulates our growth and makes us happier. The opposite mindset is avoiding relationships, and a withdrawn state that leads to isolationism, loneliness, and sadness. One in five people already live in loneliness!

Avoid conflict and drama. And yes, you can, if you choose to. How much happier and healthier we are without it. Life is far too short to spend one day, one minute, in this negativity. How often do we witness just the opposite? Check out CNN, FOX, ABC, NBC, or your local news, each day for 60 seconds or less. You'll hear about or see a lot of mental and physical abuse, social media bullying, harassment, people being victimized and threatened. Unfortunately, it's an everyday reality. Stay current with the social issues with a critical and open mind!

At this point I paused a moment and reminded my audience that once their wish is granted, they'll still be confronted by and must overcome the same day-to-day struggles and setbacks that are part of everyone's life—no one is immune or gets a waiver.

To overcome the daily doldrums, it's essential to have a feeling of purpose and meaning in our work and daily life. I've been fortunate to look forward to each day of the week focused and inspired, rather than to only live for the weekend. That's not to say each day has been terrific, but that's what has made all the tomorrows so special! Recently, on a website called InspireYourPeople.com, I read, "When something bad happens, we rise by asking, 'Now what?' When something good happens, we reach by asking, 'What's Next?'" I like this—always moving forward![63]

So, live in the present moment, savor life's gifts, and look forward to every day as if it were the weekend. Avoid drifting into the workplace chatter such as "Can't wait for the weekend," "Is it Friday yet?" or "We need another three-day weekend." Live in the present and cherish every minute of every day! You will be happy you did!

When you are completely in tune with what you are doing, you are enjoying that activity. Remember this feeling as you concentrate on one task/assignment until it is completed to the best of your ability, and you'll be happier.

In my years assigned at the Pentagon, I often had more daily work than I imagined possible to be complete. After a year of frustration and stress, I began to challenge myself daily, beginning with a written to-do list, which included everything I needed to accomplish that day. Then I prioritized the list, ranking the tasks from the easiest to the most difficult. I also allotted one hour daily for unexpected tasks from my boss and one hour for exercise. Daily exercise became a habit and reenergized me for the long afternoons.

The easier the task, the quicker it was completed, and soon I had over half the list completed before lunch. This built confidence and reduced stress. It also provided me

---

63 http://inspireyourpeople.com//internet/messages/Rise & Reach/2018

the opportunity to slow down and focus on each task, to produce quality work. At the end of the day, I normally had completed all my assigned work, had time for my coworkers, and left work content.

You can apply this or something you've developed to your schooling or employment. I often communicated to my students, "work first and play second." It's a simple thought but guarantees us greater success and ultimate happiness. Doing chores before playing videos games or using the computer, doing homework before hanging out with friends, and maintaining good eating and sleeping habits.

Students often confess their procrastination, as if it were normal behavior and humorous. Many of these same students fail classes because they don't do what's asked of them. They have poor study habits, leading to failure and unhappiness. The sad thing is that many of these same students demonstrate proficiency or better in the subject matter.

When we get to the point where learning becomes our desire and is enjoyable, something we look forward to, that's when real learning begins. It's not just learning for a grade or to pass a required test for a job application, but learning purely for passion and fulfillment. It becomes a choice. You know this, or you wouldn't be sitting here tonight.

Hopefully, you'll take your love for learning and skills

with you to college and your future careers. It will become more challenging, but you're already setting yourselves up for success.

Let me give you an example and lesson you can carry with you:

While serving at the Pentagon, I remember that one year over the course of a few days, a group of colonels made presentations to the same four-star general. This is a very high rank in the military. We only have few four-star generals. Word quickly filtered through the Pentagon halls that the general dismissed many of the colonels before they concluded their presentations. Of course, none of us were present during the briefings. As the rumors circulated, many officers no longer wanted "to take the chance" as a briefer to the general.

My questions at that time were the same as they are today:

- Were the officers well prepared to thoroughly address the subject?
- Or, did the officers believe they were prepared, giving their briefings the "routine" effort and preparation?
- Did they have clear and concise presentations, with background information, if needed?
- Were they well-rehearsed, having practiced their presentations?
- Did they develop their presentations considering that their audience was a four-star general?

- Did they anticipate the general's questions and have answers ready?
- Did they have solutions to any problems?

I suspect that the answer to any one of those questions was "probably not." They weren't prepared. If they had the opportunity for a "do over," would their presentations be different? You bet they would be. It's unwise to be ill prepared and learn this lesson at that level in the Air Force.

A few years ago, I was asked to give a Veterans Day talk, to a ladies group at a luncheon in the local community. I agreed, prepared some patriotic words, rehearsed them a few times, wore my dress blues, and off I went. My thoughts were that this would be great—lunch and the opportunity to meet some interesting women. So nice on Veterans Day.

What I failed to do was gauge my audience. Although the women were extremely cordial and wonderful hostesses, they were all elderly. Halfway through my speech, most were drifting off, and a few had fallen asleep. While I was on a roll, they were not. I remember thinking, what had I done? Clearly, I didn't know my audience and needed to cut it short and wrap it up. They awoke and thanked me. Were they thanking me for speaking or finishing?

That lesson I will never have to learn again. No matter how good a speaker you are, be well prepared and know your audience.

And lastly, I'm not going to lecture you on material wealth. Let's be real: we all have basic needs of food, shelter, and clothing, and we need money for these. In case you don't remember the levels from Psychology 101, people can't be their best possible selves (i.e., achieve self-actualization) until lower-level needs are met first.

It's difficult for people who are stressed out, have anxiety, and are struggling financially to be successful. Extreme wealth alone will never guarantee life success and happiness—examples of this truth can be found in Hollywood, professional sports, politics, and many other careers.

So for a long-term, successful, and happy life, a few commonalities exist, including our physical and emotional health. Also, we must have a desire to keep learning and growing. We all need positive relationships—nurture and enjoy these relationships. Make time in your life to enjoy your family and friends. We don't get second chances to erase regrets. Make service to others a lifelong commitment.

Before concluding, there's one more book I would like you to read. The title is *Drive: The Surprising Truth about What Motivates Us*. This book states that more than anything else, we're motivated most by a desire for autonomy, mastery, and purpose. That money is only a motivator for work that doesn't inspire passion or deep thought. And the single best motivator is our own progress and success, and the best predictor of success is our determination and perseverance.

In the end, only you will know if you're truly successful

and happy in life. You control the happiness in your life. I wish I could grant your wish tonight, but I cannot. The only person who can ... is you!

Thank – you for inviting me tonight you have been a gracious audience.

I conclude this chapter with a summary of the story, "The Black Dot."

> One day, a professor entered his classroom and asked the students to prepare for a surprise test. They all waited anxiously at their desks for the exam to begin.
>
> The professor handed out the exams and to everyone's surprise, there was no questions – just a black dot in the center of the paper. The professor, seeing the expression on everyone's faces, told them the following:
>
> "I want you to write about what you see there." The students confused, got started on the inexplicable task.
>
> At the end of the class, the professor took all the exams, and started reading each one of them out loud in the front of all the students. All of them, with no exception, defined the black dot, trying to explain its position in the center of the sheet.
>
> After all had been read, the classroom silent,

the professor started to explain:

"I'm not going to grade you on this. I just wanted to give you something to think about. No one wrote about the white part of the paper. Everyone focused on the black spot and the same thing happens in our lives. However, we insist on focusing only on the black dot — the health issues that bother us, the lack of money, the complicated relationship with a family member, the disappointment with a friend. The dark spots are very small when compared to everything we have in our lives, but they are the ones that pollute our minds. Take your eyes away from the black dots in your lives. Enjoy one of your blessings, each moment that life gives you. Be happy and live a life filled with love!"

Author Unknown

CHAPTER FIVE

Our Faith Speaks Louder than Our Words

I don't know the author, but the words are worth sharing: "No matter how sweet and kind your words are, it is your actions that loudly speak of the kind of person you are." Many quotes are like this one, and all have a similar meaning: our behavior, actions, and what we do must backup our words; otherwise, they become meaningless. Even the Bible contains a similar idea: "Dear children, let us not love with words or speech but with actions and in truth" (1 John 3:18).

I don't know about you, but it's becoming tiresome and disappointing to hear news reporters, comedians, politicians, celebrities, and others grandstand and opinionate, but follow up with little or no action or solutions to everyday challenges. Such behavior is easy, and many make a lucrative career doing it. It's hardly a benefit and service to society, though maybe it makes some people feel better, and it's entertaining. Often, this quick-to-judge chatter is cruel, demeaning, hurtful, and it alienates rather than brings people together.

Unfortunately, it has become easy to fervently believe the false and crazy daily news media. The fact is, these stories and accusations are derived from "players" on all political parties—the right, the left, and everyone else with an issue. Few are innocent and reputable. It comes down to who we *want* to believe rather than our search for the truth, regardless of what "team" we like.

Fake news and irresponsible journalism is a curse of our time. It is undermining our nation's ability to progress regarding a myriad of social justice issues. We're losing our vision and are no longer able to think for ourselves or communicate effectively. In many ways, we've become split, with conflicting stories and facts shaping our lives. In the meantime, our country suffers.

All of us need to be more attuned and think before making rapid judgements and conclusions. It's prudent and healthier for our well-being to remain silent and critically think before deriving conclusions. The truth is out there.

It hasn't always been this way. What has caused us to change? Almost anything is condoned on TV, in the news, and on social media. We're forced to accept this behavior in the politically correct world we live in and label it "freedom of speech." It doesn't appear that change will occur soon, because so much money is involved, and money talks.

What happened to professional news reporting? Obtaining facts, using credible sources, research and investigation, and validating news before publishing?

What happened to good, entertaining humor that our children could watch and read, humor that made people feel good, smile, and laugh?

What happened to the beginnings of social media and its intent, and in a short time, the infringement of privacy in our society?

What inexcusable, ill-informed talk does is affect people's lives, and cause us to question what's real from what's fake, emotion from stability. It's difficult, regardless of our education and experience in life, to determine truth from fiction, real from unreal, and assume truth. For the younger generation, who may be more susceptible and naïve, such talk can become destructive.

Free-flowing words, many untruthful and biased, cause us to distrust the source and become leery of information in general. We're trending in this direction, not in concert with justice and fairness.

We hear so many lies and see so much deceit in today's world that we've lost trust. Most people learn at a young age why this is unacceptable behavior. But many do not take this behavior into their adult lives, when it becomes more damaging. Later in life they have regrets: "If only I had ..."

Truth is strong and powerful. The beauty is that people are forgiving of others speaking and acting in truth.

Many are scared away by words from the Bible, though one might ask why, since it's the truth based on man's actions. It's one more valuable resource that all mankind can learn from. There's no need to become an extremist, live at church, or preach to others to believe in God. Find Bible passages that you relate to, and enjoy them. It's not all good news, but it speaks of all aspects of human life, and always refers us back to faith, hope, and love.

Faith means trust, confidence, assurance, and belief. Many people use the expression "Just have faith—it will work out" to encourage and comfort others in need. You'll hear people talk about it when things are good: "I knew things would turn around if I just had faith!"[64] or, "See, coach—we're winning now. All you needed was to have faith in these kids."

Faith isn't a feeling or something we feel necessary to "say" to get God to give us what we desire or to make us feel good. It doesn't work that way. It's our belief, actions, and behavior every minute of every day.

Tony Evans says the following in his article "What Is

---

64 https://newspring.cc/articles/what-does-it-mean-to-have-faith-and-why-is-it-so-important

Faith?" "Faith mostly comes down to how we view life through the lens of God's Word. Faith is perspective." He also states, "Faith means acting on what God says despite our opinions, our experience, our education. Faith is acting on the truth, whether we feel the truth or not, whether we like the truth or not, whether we *agree* with the truth or not."[65]

He uses the illustration of faith "when Jesus told Simon the fisherman to let down his nets in the deep water. Simon responded by saying that he and his companions had worked hard all night and hadn't caught anything. Then he said, "But because you say so, I will let down the nets" Luke 5:5, NIV.

Well, the fisherman got the biggest catch of their lives.

We may or may not know we have faith, and still our actions will speak louder than our words. We forgive those who hurt us, serve those in need, and respect others regardless of who they are and what they look like. Believing there is meaning and a purpose for each of us strengthens our ability to better understand and navigate through the challenges of everyday life.

According to Jacqui Griggs in her article "What Does It Mean to Have Faith—and Why Is It So Important," faith gives us three important gifts: strength, courage, and stability. You may have experienced one or more of these

---

65 http://focusonthefamily.com//internet/articles/evans/What is Faith?//

changes in your life.[66]

"Strength"

On Saturday, September 26, 1998, while assigned to Keesler Air Force Base, Biloxi, Mississippi, we were notified that Hurricane Georges was heading to the coast expected to hit on the 28th. With over 12,000 military, civilian, and family members assigned and hundreds living on the base, we evacuated all military personnel and their families from base housing and strongly suggested they depart the area. "Essential" military remained on base. If families opted to remain on base, bunkered facilities were available; however, they'd be responsible for their own personal belongings, food, medicine, etc.

On Sunday, the storm arrived as predicted. Gusty winds were recorded up to 125 mph, power was quickly out, and boats were plucked out of the water and dropped on the base shorelines. It was dark and loud, then quiet with green and blue flashes of light in the sky, and then dark again. The rain and winds were intense. The hurricane circled us.

On Tuesday, September 29, the storm had passed. The base was still closed; the damage was done. What was four days seemed like four weeks to me, concerned with the welfare of my family, who had departed, and all our troops and their families.

Amazingly, we had no fatalities or major injuries,

---

66 http://newspring.cc//internet/article/jacqui Griggs/What does it mean to have faith – and why is it so important?//

---

considering the number of military, civilians, and family members assigned to Keesler AFB. Also, the hundreds of family members who remained in the bunkers with their children were outstanding. Their courage and strength was extraordinary. While visiting the families during the storm, I remember a much calmer feeling than expected—just the usual "When do you think it will be over?" and "When can we go home?" The children seemed happy playing with friends, experiencing something new.

This family faith gave me strength through those long days and nights.

"Courage"

Per Grigg's article, "Courage is the ability to do what scares us, to act on our beliefs despite threats of danger, to show strength in [the] face of grief or pain. Courage, like strength, comes directly from our faith in God."[67]

A story I like about courage involves Irena Sendler in World War II.

When the Nazis invaded her native Poland, and rounded up all the Jews into a walled-in prison, Sendler knew she must be a person of action. She knew that the lives of many innocent imprisoned depended on her and few others. What she accomplished was amazing. It's estimated that Sendler and her group helped get approximately 2500 children out of the prison using her truck —and sent them through a

---

67 *Http://newspring.cc//internet/article/Jacqui Griggs/What does it mean to have faith – and why is it so important?//*

network of comrades to Christian orphanages, where they were given new identities. She kept their real names in a jar buried in the backyard.

Sendler was eventually caught by the Nazis, who imprisoned and tortured her. When the war ended she devoted herself to reuniting children with their families.[68]

"Stability"

Griggs states, "Faith in God is what allows us to experience stability in the middle of instability. When life feels out of control, we take comfort in knowing that God is in control."[69] When I read this, mothers come to my mind. They deal with instability daily, and most do it unselfishly, with many duties, daily chaos, and responsibility.

George W. Bush once said, "I think you can judge from somebody's actions a kind of stability and sense of purpose perhaps created by strong religious roots. I mean, there's a certain patience, a certain discipline, I think, that religion helps you achieve."

When I was a 23-year-old in Air Force Officer Training School and a few weeks away from graduation, all of us cadets were given a personality test. Soon after, we were provided the results, with our personalities and aptitudes. In a dark, drab auditorium called the blue room, our instructor provided each of us the name(s) of historic military leaders

68 http://newspring.cc//internet/article/jacqui Griggs/What does it mean to have faith – and why is it so important?//
69 http://newspring.cc//internet/article/jacqui Griggs/What does it mean to have faith – and why is it so important?//

who had similar personalities. I waited patiently for my turn.

A few cadets received two names, and for some reason I was one of the last cadets called. I remember thinking, maybe there was no name for me—maybe I was "unworthy." And then I heard, "Matera, General George Patton Jr." We all did the same thing upon class dismal: went to the barracks and quietly researched our leaders.

I was awestruck. I didn't know General Patton and had a different perception of him. After reviewing General Patton, my confidence soared, and I felt stronger regarding my personality and aptitude for military service. I was happy to have General Patton in my hip pocket for the next 25 years.

What I learned was that General Patton, unknown to many in the public, was humble, people oriented, and a man of faith. He was a religious man, and his faith in God was strong through failures and successes. To be successful, Patton believed in being well prepared, to work hard and pray. His focus was always completing the mission while also caring for his soldiers. Courage and victory—he never lost sight of these goals. He required his troops to work hard, be loyal to one another, devoted to duty, and have courage, and in return he gave them his leadership, compassion, and trust.

Michael Keane, author of *Patton: Blood, Guts and Prayer*, discusses General Patton in an interview, saying, "'For this guy, faith was part of his being. ... If you ignore

Patton's Christianity, then you cannot understand how he approached challenges or how he achieved his successes, or how he shaped history.'" Keane goes on to say, "'He was raised reading the Bible, praying every day. ... His faith in God and his faith in himself became this core.'" General Patton was very devoted. Keane says that prayer "wasn't just a gimmick to him. What you start to understand is that Patton saw prayer as a force, a force of nature, a force of God, really, not just some words uttered. He thought that everyone praying together was like a force field, like an X-ray, you couldn't see it, but it could shape and affect things, with power unto itself ... That's why he had the whole Third Army pray and issue a directive on prayer because he thought it would help them accomplish their mission."[70]

General Patton transferred his faith to his men. His men knew he cared for them; he showed it throughout his career. Having faith didn't diminish his qualities as a soldier. He was tough, brave, and courageous. He led from the front, unlike many other military leaders. His leadership is an example of how actions speak louder than words.

On December 22, 1944, General Patton ordered that the following prayer, with his own short holiday greeting, be published and distributed to his troops in the Third Army:

"Almighty and most merciful Father, we humbly beseech Thee, of Thy great goodness, to restrain these immoderate rains with which we have had to contend. Grant us fair

70 www.Patton: Blood, Guts and Prayer //text/Keane/2012

weather for Battle. Graciously hearken to us as soldiers who call upon Thee that armed with Thy power, we may advance from victory to victory, and crush the oppression and wickedness of our enemies, and establish Thy justice among men and nations. Amen."[71]

The German and American meteorologists had agreed that there would be three weeks of rain. So, it seemed a miracle when the sun rose into a cloudless sky on the morning of December 23.

General Patton addressed the Third Army, somewhere in England June 5th, 1944. It was a critical time frame dampening Germany's thoughts of surging and winning the war. His words were simple, impactful and that of a leader demanding loyalty and excellence. He told his troops they were there for three reasons: "to defend your homes and loved ones, for your own self-respect, because you would not want to be anywhere else, and last, because you are real soldiers and men." He went on to speak of team work, the importance of each man doing his job with pride "even to the one who heats our water."

Never in my 25 years of service have I heard a general officer talk so compassionately to his troops the way General Patton did. He was immensely patriotic, a man of faith, the same faith his men absorbed, and determined to lead his country to victory.

---

71 http://historyonthenet.com//internet/articles/When Patton Enlisted the Entire Third Army to Pray for Fair Weather/Ref: Patton: Blood, Guts, and Prayer 2012 by Michael Keane

After reading, "Killing Patton," by Bill O'Reilly and Martin Dugard, I realized I would have loved to serve with General Patton. Why not, we had the same personality. Though there was the realization the general's expectations would be the highest and failure was not an option. Our country's security and safety was his priority and we would do it together...each one of us, with no guarantee of fairness but ultimate justice.

Having served in my own military career, my faith has never wavered. However, that hasn't stopped me from questioning my religion at times, and searching for answers.

For example, I've always questioned a part of The Lord's Prayer, also known as the "Our Father." An excerpt from the newer version is: "Give us today the food we need, and forgive us our sins, as we have forgiven those who sin against us."[72]

How can we be expected to forgive others who have inflicted such pain and harm on us?

Why should we be asked to do so?

If forgiveness is God's expectation, why have we so repeatedly failed him? God, why do you ask this of us?

I continue to pray, and in my own mind know God's word is truth. Who am I to question it? Honestly, in this case, it was my own weakness that caused skepticism. It has taken me many years to come to peace with myself and God on this issue. My faith is sustained.

72 http://lords-prayer-words.com//internet/prayers/TheLord's Prayer(NLT)

Alexandra Asseily said, "Forgiveness allows us to let go of the pain in the memory and if we let go of the pain in the memory we can have the memory but it does not control us. When memory controls us we are then the puppets of the past."[73]

How many people do you know who are unwilling to forgive? Family members, ex-spouses, coworkers, friends, neighbors, etc. They haven't spoken for days, months, maybe years.

They harbor anger, sorrow, righteousness, so many emotions that they've imprisoned themselves from living with faith and the grace of forgiveness. Something special is taken from us when we're unwilling to forgive. Our faith and love is restored when we do.

The negative emotions that come with holding grudges involves carrying stress responses in our body. Over time, this can impact our overall health. Researchers at Emory University have shown that holding stress contributes to high blood pressure and heart disease. Holding grudges and not being able to forgive results in stress. Healthy people avoid this limitation.

Many amazing stories about forgiveness can inspire. Once such story is about a woman named Pascale Kavanagh, who was abused by her mother. As an adult, Kavanagh never intended to rekindle a relationship with her mother. But things changed in 2010: "her mother suffered several

[73] http://csmonitor.com//internet/articles/Amy Green/At Virginia Tech, a film asks, 'can we forgive?'/09212007//

strokes that left her unable to communicate or take care of herself. With no one else to help, Kavanagh began to sit by her mother's bedside and read to her. Through this, Kavanagh says the hate she had for her mother dissipated into forgiveness and love."[74]

I've asked God if forgiving but remembering is faith. Honestly, I knew the answer before asking. We cannot compromise our faith.

When we check what's in our hearts, we'll know. Be the first to give a hug, to make a call, or visit. It's not always easy, but we're often surprised by what we find on the other side.

Forget what someone has done to you, and forgive forever. Learn to forgive. We'll live in an atmosphere of internal peace and love, rather than darkness and negativity. It seems human to harbor the wrongs others inflict on us; however, we do have a choice.

If the issue of forgiveness applies to you, as it does to many, mark a date on your calendar, and make the commitment to resolve the issue. In the end, you gain strength and unleash a tremendous burden. You have nothing to lose and much to gain.

Former President Bill Clinton once asked Nelson Mandela how he had forgiven those who'd kept him wrongly imprisoned for so long. Mandela answered, "I didn't want

---

74 http://realsimple.com//internet/articles/Ayling/I Forgave my Mother for Abusing Me

to be in prison anymore. Of course I felt old anger rising up again, and fear. After all, I had not been free in 27 years. But I knew that, when I drove away from the gate, if I continued to hate them, they would still have me. I wanted to be free, and so I let it go."[75] Imagine if we all knew of this example and were able to apply it in our lives. So much happier we would be!

While talking to myself recently, I asked, "Can a person have faith without belief in God?"

It seems that we can trust and love others, and show loyalty and devotion here on earth. Then I realized this didn't answer the question.

Faith isn't something we're born with and can turn on and off. Faith is a gift from God and God only, to each of us. It's our choice to follow God and accept and use this gift. Therefore, we cannot possess faith without belief in the one who gave it to us. Then I asked, if this is such an important gift in life, one no amount of money can buy, why are there non-believers? Because they haven't seen or felt?

Often in life, like the soldier in the foxhole, our faith surfaces when faced with adversity and challenge. So is the case of Steve Scalise, House majority whip, who has recently recovered from injuries sustained in the June 2017 shooting in Alexandria, Virginia, and returned to work.

According to Lissandra Villa, a BuzzFeed news reporter,

---

75 http://vanityfair.com//internet/articles/Bill Clinton/A Man Called Hope//12092013

Sept 28, 2017, the Louisiana Representative has returned to work at the Capitol.

Scalise spoke to his fellow congressmen when he entered the chamber, thanking them and the public for their love and support. He said, "'It's given us the strength to get through all of this.' He also spoke of his faith, saying that his prayers were answered. 'I'm definitely a living example that miracles really do happen,' he said."

The congressman also responded to how he felt the experience had changed him: "'Yes, it changed me, but not in the ways you might think ... It's only strengthen my faith in God and its really crystalized what shows up in the goodness of people. ... To me, all I remember are the thousands of acts of kindness that came out of this. ... [It] helped me realize just how wonderful most people are and just how much compassion is out here.'"[76]

In my life I've been fortunate to not have to see or feel to believe, although at times I have questioned. Having faith in God doesn't exempt us from life's challenges...I consider it God's will, to see how we respond in our actions and deeds. Do we falter and give up, or continue stronger in life?

After the unexpected loss of my younger sister a few years ago, my family recently placed my 93-year-old father in a nursing home. Dad was 90 years old at the time,

---

76 http://BuzzFeed.Inc//internet/articles/Lissandra Villa/Steve Scalise Returns to the Capitol After Months of Recovering From Alexandria Shooting/09282017

had been diagnosed with severe dementia, had a memory comparable to that of a young child, and had the body of a man 20 years younger. He no longer knew us, couldn't take care of himself, and was becoming delusional.

He loved his home and landscaping his yard. He was the street mayor—a proud man who cared for others, still mowing, snow plowing, and cutting trees for neighbors. He would pick up the debris and load it in his old Ford Ranger truck, and to the dump he'd go. Sometimes two or three times a day. The neighbors let him be mayor, knowing his joy. He loved his "friends." There was no way he was ever leaving.

One day while on the top step of a ladder with an electric saw, cutting a neighbor's tree, he fell, and the saw slipped and entered his quadricep muscle to the bone. Fortunately, the neighbor was home and got him to a hospital. In a few months he rehabbed and continued his neighborhood service, but he'd never be the same. We knew that for his safety and well-being it was time to move him somewhere, to a safe and pleasant environment.

My mother, older sister, and brother all agreed from the start that it was the best decision and the most humane thing to do. I resisted and wrestled with this decision. If he loved living life so much in his own home, doing his own thing, why should we deprive him in his last few years of life? I considered other medical options in his home. After making phone calls, talking with agencies in state and county services, the options ran out.

In the end, I trusted my family, had faith in their wishes, and considered what was best for any human being in this situation, let alone my dad. Then looking to my God, I prayed one last time. Our decision should be what was best for my dad, not what I wanted. Our family agreed—acting on faith. My brother and I placed him in home care. It was a difficult day in my life, but with faith it was possible, providing him a safe haven with peace and comfort.

Our family's faith is stronger than words. My mother instilled this in us over a life time, but as kids and young adults we had no idea of this gift's value. We've been tested, and with prayer and faith, we're stronger.

My father enlisted in the Marine Corps at the age of 18, primarily to provide for his poor family. He later transferred into the Air Force, became a fighter pilot, and flew in the Korean War. He served his country for 50-plus years and rose to the rank of major general. He had devout love and faith for his country and all people who served, regardless of who they were and where they came from.

On occasion my father would say to me, "Gene, there are no atheists in foxholes." Reflecting on the times he'd spoken these words, I realized they were muttered after I screwed up—a teacher called home, a citizenship flaw, or after missing a first communion practice. Something went wrong, and he wanted me to get back on track. His faith was different than our mother's, but who was I to judge?

During my Air Force career, I found this saying truer than not. Sure, there were atheists in the service. However, I never thought about it or cared. Until one day, when the commander of the base I was assigned to gave a small cadre of us a directive to go home, get our bags, and report back at X hours that evening. We were deploying, without further information.

When we were airborne in a C-130 aircraft on a cold night in pitch-black skies, not knowing the destination and what our mission was, I noticed two airmen sitting across from me reading Bibles. No sound, no emotion, totally transcended. They were courageous young men, seemingly for the moment, without fear. I then remembered my father's words and wished I had a Bible. Their actions spoke louder than anything they could have said, and their action made me want to pray.

Real faith motivates us to action. We demonstrate living faith by what we do and not what we say. Think about this as you do your daily reflections and observe others around you.

Even research supports my father's words. When Cornell University behavioral economist Brian Wansink studied World War II post-combat surveys, he discovered that during heavy combat, the number of soldiers who relied on prayer increased from 42% to 72%.[77] I'll assume historical analysis of more recent conflicts is close to these

77 http://news.cornell.edu/stories/2013/05/no-atheists-foxholes-wwii-vets-remain-religious

same numbers. A 30% increase of people turn to prayer while facing stressful and life-threatening experiences. I'll also assume that approximately 70% of all people in an environment facing the reality of death reach out for their faith. It would be interesting to determine the real numbers.

In George Washington's 1796 farewell address he stated, "that religion and morality are indispensable to America's happiness, reality, prosperity and totally to its success. It is our faith and our values that inspires us to give with charity, to act with courage, and to sacrifice for what we know is right."[78]

We seem to be living in a time where public prayer and displays of faith are often criticized and attacked. In some schools, community functions, and events the Pledge of Allegiance or national anthem has been eliminated. A far cry from the hopes and dreams of the people who fought and died for the country we live in today. Should not all Americans have the right to practice and show their faith, without harassment and/or persecution?

A recent memorable display of public prayer occurred during an NFL game between the San Francisco 49ers and New York Giants. Marquise Goodwin, a 49ers wide receiver, showed his faith, not by demonstrating, beating his chest after a catch, or looking for the limelight. After scoring a touchdown, Goodwin kneeled in the end zone. He did this to pay tribute to his wife, because they'd lost

---

78 http://www.wnd.com/2017/10/trump-in-america-we-dont-worship-government/.

their son at birth two days earlier. Speaking about the experience, Goodwin said:

> Honest to God truth, the only reason I made it through the game is because of my faith in God. ... I mentally and physically was not prepared to play in the game—at all. I really didn't even practice that week, I was just going through a lot. ... Coming into the game, I wasn't really in it because I had just lost my baby. My wife, we prayed about it and I guess she felt that God moved her to allow me to go play and she encouraged me. She raised my spirits up and helped me get ready for the game. ... So, situations like that, you only make it through that with your faith in God.[79]

As Goodwin's story relates, to have faith is to believe in something, and to trust. Some people believe everything they're told. Others require proof for everything. Most people cannot profess faith in something unless they have knowledge regarding it.

It's an unhealthy quality to believe in things of which we have no proof, facts, or verification. It's astounding how often we see this today. Immediate belief in something that often is untrue or has a magnitude of issues attached to it, necessitating further knowledge and reason.

One way to overcome this emotional state is to stop

79 http://www.espn.com/nfl/story/_/id/21415238/san-francisco-49ers-wide-receiver-marquise-goodwin-discusses-loss-child

ourselves, disregard the rapid-fire words we hear, and listen and search for meaning and truth. In a sense, we become well informed and use our strength to develop our own beliefs. We should teach all children this simple practice. Think for yourself, listen to others, and derive your own beliefs—it demands our compassion for and acceptance of others. Having an open heart and mind is truly a gift for a life time.

Not long ago, CNN posted data from the Southern Poverty Law Center, which states that 917 active hate groups now operate in the U.S. In reviewing this data, a few things stuck out to me. First the overall high number, and that they operate in nearly every state and represent many different religions, races, and political systems.

As adults, we're responsible for ensuring that our youth are aware of and educated regarding these groups—who they are, what their purposes and beliefs are, and why they act with prejudice, hate, and fear. It should be our goal that no child enlists with these groups, that no child be brainwashed or coerced, that no child be lost in this hell. Young adults can drift and are often susceptible to "greener pastures."

Teaching youth to think for themselves and develop their own beliefs and faith is primarily accomplished in the family, in school, with peers, and at church, in this order. We don't require a Harvard psychology degree to conclude this. I placed the church last in this list because more children attend school on a regular basis for a longer duration of time than they do church. I hope the good sisters and lay teachers at Edgewood High School, my alma mater, understand my logic, and won't delete my photo from their yearbook collection.

Parenting is the responsibility to raise healthy, mature, and responsible children. When this occurs, great. When it doesn't, we must examine the parenting, or the lack of it. It's clear that the family structure in our country has changed over the past few decades, for better or worse, and which issues are causing the changes are debatable.

Good parenting is tough, and even the "best" parents are imperfect. In most cases, they made a choice to have children, and thus accepted the corresponding responsibilities. Good parents don't consider how much better their lives would be without children. They work hard, preparing their children to be good citizens. They are loving, caring, and responsible. They hold their children accountable but at the same time are patient. They are home for their children and spend quality time with them. They communicate honestly with their children. They listen to and value their children's opinions. They are consistent and fair. They are involved in their children's lives. And there is faith, hope, and love in the home.

Parenting is challenging and becomes more so in a single-parent family. According to a *New York Times* article, in 1968, about 8.3 million American children lived in a single-parent home. By 2015, that number increased to almost 20 million, or 27% of all children 18 years old and younger. Those living with two parents fell from 86% to 69%. In a summary of the findings, the article also says, "Children living with a single parent tend to do worse in life than those who grow up in a stable two-parent family."[80]

More and more parents have careers, placing greater demands on their daily schedules. I've seen many teens leaving and/or returning home without parenting. My observations of many of these children's daily welfare and happiness aren't optimistic.

I'm concerned for our youth, their welfare and opportunities to lead successful, happy lives instilled with faith. Call it my age, but I've seen it in person. When children live in the home prior to adulthood, their well-being and needs must come first. Schools, churches, and peers, all provide necessary influences for a child's growth and welfare, but they do not and never will substitute for effective parenting.

Years ago, parents often believed it was the church's job to teach their children religion. But today we know that if a child has any chance of growing up with faith, it's because of the parents. These years go by fast, and this is the precious time to bond with your child and grow together. Parents are their children's best example—lead them, teach them, love them.

---

80 *http://nytimes.com//internet/articles/Russell &Porter/Living With One Parent/03222016*

Our faith isn't passive—it's active. It's not waiting for God to do something for me, but me taking the first steps toward my own beliefs and faith. What am I doing about my own faith? "God helps those who help themselves" to the extent that our motives align with God's will. Are we living our life purely for ourselves or considering others and God? We can apply this faith in many aspects of our lives.

It's like the person who's filled with sorrow and pain and wants to have hope, but withdraws and quits on life. He has nothing to hold onto—no faith, hope, or love in his heart. No one wants to be this person; unfortunately, many are. No person is denied forgiveness and new life if they possess faith. Forgiveness is one of mankind's great gifts.

Faith can do a lot of things in our life, if we let it. It helps us grow in a healthy, happier life, with inner peace and strength. Faith makes us people of action, with little need or use for words. We have confidence in what we hope for and the courage to act on our beliefs. We are then at peace with ourselves and the world around us.

Research shows that religion and spirituality can help people cope with major life stressors, including serious substance abuse and mental illness, according to the American Psychiatric Association. In other words, there's power in believing in a higher power and sometimes, it's even the starting place for getting help.

Faith based organizations are rising and providing a viable option in our health care system. They provide alternative treatment for people with major life stressors, including serious mental health, according to the American Psychiatric Association.

CHAPTER SIX

Life Is Constantly Changing

Life moves forward, always changing. I mentioned earlier that change is good, but that's not a guarantee. With change comes risk and uncertainty. For this reason, many skeptics fear change. In fact, change is mankind's number one fear, more fear inducing than death itself. When we realize we have no control over change and begin to accept the idea, we move forward.

We should never forget our history—our culture, customs, and traditions—but at the same time we should seek to foster our own growth and others' quality of life.

Change can result in many different emotions, including anxiety and fear. When someone broadcasts, "We're going to change ...,"and we hear it for the first time, our faces redden, barriers go up, and we can become resistant.

Then, after absorbing the shock, we exclaim things like the following: "Why change? Everything is going well." "Why reinvent the wheel?" "We know what we're doing—we were here long before they showed up."

Our experiences with success and failure influence our emotions. At times in our lives, having failed repeatedly, we're naturally inclined to give up and quit. "We've tried this a hundred times, and it doesn't work." This attitude causes us to build barriers before fully considering the change. Ironically, the proposed change may be the very thing we need in life.

When we encounter unwelcome change, the best approach is to obliterate our emotions and objectively examine the change. Ask ourselves, if the change will occur, how do I become an integral person to support team members and achieve the best goal? If the change is questionable, become the person who leads the discussion and works to determine its viability. In both cases you're proactive and a positive force in the resolution process, rather than someone with emotional baggage. It's our choice.

When it comes to change, we may not be able to control the outcome, but we can control our response to the change. Our attitude and thought processes determine our ability to handle change and the uncertainty that goes with it. Being open minded, confident, and positive aids decision making. We can transform changes into opportunities.

We don't progress in life by sharing our emotions and feelings with words like, "This is the way I/we feel; therefore, it must change." Healthy progression in our lives simply doesn't work this way. Change in life can be difficult, require hard work, and often involves other people, and their needs and feelings.

To overcome possible stress and an overwhelming feeling, Jane Burnett provides a list called "6 Ways to Embrace Change at Work and at Home": "Think about the important things in life ... Put Your Mental and Physical Health First ... Cut back where you can ... Focus on what you can control ... Talk to someone you really care about ... [and] Appreciate the little things."[81]

Change is challenging for both the initiators and receivers. It isn't easy to sell change to others and then to implement and support it. We must understand that change will occur in nearly all of our daily activities, whether we like it or not.

Attitude is powerful in life. Imagine if we could instill this in all our youth. Positive people enjoy life more and are generally happier and more successful. People gravitate toward positive people and distance themselves from the pessimistic. Why do many not see this?

I often told my students that I have always, without a second thought, hired a person with a good attitude and good qualifications over another with a questionable

81 http://theladders.com//internet/articles/Jane Burnett/6 ways to embrace change at work and at home/09102017

attitude with brilliant credentials. A person with a poor attitude infects others; a person with a good attitude inspires and motivates. Most people can be trained to perform job duties; we can't train attitude.

While we're all born with certain personality traits, we shape our own attitudes through our relationships and experiences. Our attitudes begin to develop in early childhood and constantly change over the years, into adult life. Therefore, the family has the strongest impact on children's attitudes, and this responsibility shouldn't be outsourced. Unfortunately, it too often is, and some parents don't even realize they're doing it.

No secrets here—I had more than my fair share of attitude adjustments growing up. Thankfully, I had people around me who cared and took the time to teach and guide me. They were honest with me. I refer to it as "tough love." My parents, a few of the coaches and good sisters in school, and my peers made a difference in my life. We're not all this fortunate.

At times, it hurt. The lessons were painful, and the time-outs and "groundings" seemed endless. My attitude changes were evident, and eventually I felt success.

With the need to change, some will be in denial and withdraw. They accept their pessimistic and grumpy life and consider others the culprits for their state of mind. If one is unable or unwilling to face their denial, change is impossible. This is a time when a trusting confidant is needed, to speak truth. This is often difficult, but in the end rewarding. It's like getting an alcoholic to accept his or her addiction and attend weekly meetings, and ultimately overcome their addiction. We all need honest and constructive coaching in our lives.

Too often we're indifferent to being truthful with others. Helping to correct people's weaknesses is caring for and loving them, yet we're reluctant to do so. We think it's not our business, we don't have the time and desire, or we believe interfering will affect our relationships. Neither giving or receiving constructive criticism is ever easy, but by doing so we stimulate our personal growth and professional development. In essence, we fulfill this need for others.

As a junior officer in the Air Force, I consistently received outstanding evaluations and comments. I quickly realized my own strengths and weaknesses, though they were rarely discussed. What I eventually sought out was constructive feedback to further my improvement. Maybe others more senior and experienced saw things in my performance that I didn't. Performance feedback needs to be real, honest, and constructive.

My high-school football coach mentored me through the teen years, and I never realized it. He was tough, fair, and encouraging, in his own way. He had an eye on me every minute of the school day, let me know it, and kept me on the straight and narrow. He once told me, "If I wasn't talking with you, I wouldn't be caring for you." He believed in the best possible me, and that made me want to live up to his belief.

Everyone can use a mentor as they progress through life. Find your own, a person you trust, who inspires and encourages you. Don't be afraid to confront this person and reach out.

While we're in the process of changing our attitudes, we need to visualize how this change will make us a more positive and productive person. What exactly is it that I'm aiming for? Healthier relationships, greater opportunities in my career? Is it for my children and family, my social life?

Having a goal and passion to succeed will help make this attitudinal change occur. Our goals should begin "I will," "I can," or "I must," rather than "I think I can," "Maybe I will," or "I will try." The same positive thinking applies to any goal we set for ourselves.

During the recent school year, the school district and then our high-school principal asked 141 of the teachers to examine our grading practices. We needed to collaborate amongst our departments and determine if any positive changes could be made to improve the grading system. An enormous amount of information and research was provided to the teachers, showing strengths and weaknesses of nationwide grading policies. Our grading by department was provided to the entire staff. All schools in the district were asked to comply.

There was good news and challenges along the way.

Did all teachers positively accept this assignment and embrace it? No.

Were some resistant to the exercise and question of change? Yes.

Did teachers begin the exercise with the goal of collaborating with the administration to determine positive changes we could make to grading practices? No.

We spent an inordinate amount of time wrestling with negative mindsets, and a feeling that we were being chastised as teachers. Many viewed the administration as more concerned with student achievement than our hard work, experience, and expertise. That wasn't the case at all, but many teachers became emotional. It just didn't seem fair!

Nevertheless, it was a relevant and worthwhile exercise, and the process was a good lesson in and of itself. I recently retired from teaching, and I don't know if any changes were implemented.

We wasted time and fought change. If we teachers had initially not seen this as questioning our professionalism and the "way we have been grading forever," and instead examined the reasons for this exercise, we may have developed ideas and recommendations, or even proposed changes that could be standardized and implemented.

Teachers are educated and resourceful. They don't just go with the flow or change something they know nothing about. However, even positive change can be stalled or discarded, and we don't even know it.

Sometime later, teacher leadership began to develop, committees and groups were formed, and action began. Teachers were conversing with one another and the administration, and about that time, school ended for the summer. My hope is that the teachers will be proactive this year, rekindled with enthusiasm regarding this subject, and make it one of their success stories. It is, after all, what is best for the students.

This is an example of a negative attitude that needed to be changed. The possibilities may be tremendous. It's worth the time for all of us to reflect and determine who we are. Are we negative, the habitual complainer, and the worrier? Do we live our life always looking over our shoulders, with fear and distrust? Do our barriers go up at the first sign of possible change, and what's our immediate reaction? "I don't believe in this. I'm not spending my time on it." If so, we may have behaved like this for so long that we no longer see who we are. This behavior can be changed, if we want to change it.

Most would agree that they want to be productive and proactive regarding changes in their lives, though they're occasionally held back. It's important to let go of our stresses and anxiety, which is sometimes easier said than done. The sooner we set aside our burdens and problems, the sooner we can move forward.

Not all change is productive and good. Numerous ideas, recommendations, and suggestions have failed to produce change. Many of the changes in our lives occurred after repeated failure. And when we failed, we persevered. Sometimes our ideas won't work and aren't accepted.

At this point, it's important that we remain positive for the next opportunity. The small risk we take is worth the reward. Life provides many wonderful opportunities to initiate personal change.

Leslie Becker–Phelps, in her article "Knowing When to Accept and When to Change," puts it this way: "The serenity prayer offers great wisdom. While there is much to appreciate in the ability to be accepting *and* in the ability to busily work to make changes, these qualities are not enough. A greater virtue is to know when to engage each of them—and then, of course, to proactively do so." She goes on to say it is the "'wisdom to know the difference'" that many people struggle with.[82]

Change is constantly occurring everywhere. Each of us are changing, in addition to our children, friends, families, workplaces, and society. It's a challenge to balance and make sense of it daily, particularity if the change directly involves us. And where would we be without it? We need change.

A few significant and wonderful changes come to my mind: the fall of the Berlin Wall in Germany, cures for many

82 *http://psychologytoday.com//internet/articles/Leslie Becker–Phelps PH.D./Knowing When to Accept and When to Change/06282017*

illnesses and diseases, recovering drug and alcohol addicts, improved care for our elderly and disabled, the advent of the internet and its use for all people, and our country's progress regarding equality and justice.

All of these changes took an enormous amount of time and work. Even change for equality is ongoing, and we continue to move toward the one day all people will parade together with joy and happiness, without fear of violence and hatred.

We're much more productive in life when extracting the question of fairness from our lives and dedicate our energy to social justice. Fairness revolves around me and I; justice encompasses we and us. One is self-serving, the other serves and cares for others. In justice we can influence change; we have little control over fairness.

Consider the case in which many talented executives were working for a major car manufacturer. The company develops, manufactures, and sells cars and trucks. The CEO isn't working well with his executives. He has recently dismissed many in leadership positions. His staff feels he is aloof, isn't communicating, and is making decisions without confiding and collaborating with them. The executives are unaware of decision making and feel blindsided. They are frustrated and often angry, searching for honesty and openness. Morale in the company has been on the decline. The stock price in the company has been on a decrease the past 12 months.

Many of the executives have considered leaving the company. They're torn between resigning or staying for the good of the company–a company with which they have significant experience and expertise. They realize if many leave it may impact the company.

The decision process can be extremely difficult, but better thought–out over time. Sleep on it a few days or so, and you may find out your decision is different, and one you will not regret. The final decision must be what is best for you and your family."

As these employees reflect, a few questions come to mind: Am I making an impact and using all my talents and experience? Is my voice and work still respected and well received? Am I vital to moving the company forward? Am I still passionate, and do I still enjoy my job? If an employee answers yes to these questions, he or she is likely to stay.

If on the other hand, the employees cannot work with the present style of decision making, closed door leadership, fear for their reputations, or any moral issues resulting in their inability to perform, they will leave.

The case above, with teachers being asked to evaluate their grading practices, involved institutional change. The automobile company and its employees involves career changes. Most of us change careers in our lives for different reasons, and it's often a daunting and difficult experience.

The above illustrations are but a finite number of changes we face in a lifetime. Everything changes, and there is always change. The way to handle life's change is difficult to teach children. As we grow, we begin to understand that we must be able to adjust to change, whether that change is negative or positive.

Even the smallest changes in our lives can appear huge and overwhelming. No two people will face the same changes in their lives and adjust similarly. This is normal. We shouldn't compare our thoughts and feelings to those of others. There is no right or wrong way.

These thoughts brought back memories of a personality evaluation I provided my freshman classes each year. The evaluation uses four colors: gold, green, blue, and orange. Each color/personality has character traits, likes and dislikes, their responses in life, pictures, etc. I provided each student with each personality's characteristics, and I then gave them time to evaluate themselves by providing percentages for each personality type, to equal 100%.

When they were ready, the students would go to one of the classroom's four corners, based on their number one color/personality. The goals were to show each student their personalities, as well as how each person is important to everyone else, and how we could use this knowledge to build a stronger and more cohesive class. Furthermore, and most importantly, that we need people of all personalities to coexist. It was a fun exercise that the students enjoyed, and they remembered their personalities throughout high school.

One day, not long after we'd conducted the personality evaluation, a freshman boy came to my office. He told me he wanted to enter the Marine Corps upon graduation. He was concerned that if he joined the Marines, they'd change his personality, and he didn't want that to happen. I remember thinking, "Wow, what insight for a 14-year-old—the thought of someone or something changing who he was." How long had he been thinking about this?

I told him that no one can change another person's personality. Our primary personality traits and who we are will never change, but the percentages of the colors will change, as we continue to grow. He was relieved and smiled as if I had lifted a tremendous burden. Three years later, he enlisted in the Marine Corps.

As Salini Nair's poem "Change" says, "Change is a change to know the real self."[83]

---

83 *http://poemlist.com//internet/poemlist/Salini Nair/Change –Poem/2014*

CHAPTER SEVEN

Hope Is Our Only Choice

"You never know how strong you are until being strong is the only choice you have." —Unknown

Excerpts from the story, "The Dying Boy"

One day a hospital program teacher was assigned to visit a child in the hospital and help him keep up with his school work.

The teacher immediately conversed with the child's regular teacher and then went to see the boy. The teacher was unaware that the boy had been badly burned and was in great pain. Taken back at the sight of the boy she told him, "I've been sent by your school to help you with your school work." She left the boy feeling low that she had not accomplished much.

The next day, a nurse asked her, "What did you do with that boy? Since yesterday, his whole attitude has changed. He's fighting back, responding to treatment. It's as though he's decided to live."

Two weeks later the boy explained he had given up hope until the teacher arrived. He expressed it this way, "They wouldn't send a teacher to work ...with a dying boy, would they?"

Our hope can be lost, and just as quickly we can find it again. Sometimes all it can take is someone else's simple act of compassion, or a caring attitude that uplifts us. In the case of the dying boy, assume he felt lost and forgotten until someone cared and visited. It's a reminder to all of mankind the power of Hope and to never give up on ourselves and others.

Each of us is capable of inspiring others, if we want to. There are no qualifications or experience necessary—only our caring for others before ourselves. Sometimes, our actions can infuse a person's life with renewed hope.

Hope isn't a feeling or emotion. It's not wishing the Packers will win on Sunday, that the teacher doesn't give us a test today, or that it won't rain when we don't want it to. It's not a wish or dream. For me, it's easiest to understand hope as the ability to see that there is light, despite all the darkness around us.

My younger brother is an engineer and quality manager for Ford Motor Company. He's intelligent, passionate, and dedicated to his job. He is also caring and compassionate for those working with him. He supervises with high expectations, a sense of humor, and many hours of hard work. He is first on and last off the engine assembly line. His employees look forward to work; they know they'll succeed, in a teamwork environment.

Recently, I asked him what he thought regarding the topics for this book. Misunderstanding—or with humor—he texted: "In this order 1) justice 2) faith 3) It's not fair 4) hope. Just a side note, a quality manager never hopes ... he knows!"

I read his message at 5:30 a.m., while having coffee and ready to go to the gym. I wondered, "Who schooled who here?" I let it go, figuring he was already working and didn't need any of my distractions. Then another thought came to mind: maybe he sees hope differently and needs clarification.

Later in the day I was enlightened by his follow-up text: "We are a multicultural society, and too often we embarrass it. Too often we do not take the time to appreciate others and their beliefs. Yes, the work needs to get done—pilots must fly, we must drive our cars, engines must be shipped, kids need to be taught ... when we take the time to really learn and respect one another, whether it be a coworker, neighbor, a quality engineer in China, will we ever be successful."

I responded with a thumbs-up. He definitely will get a copy of this book.

An example of living with hope is a story of Viktor Frankl, a former prisoner in a Nazi prison camp, who had the following epiphany while digging a trench: "In a last violent protest against the hopelessness of imminent death, I sensed my spirit piercing through the enveloping gloom. I felt it transcend that hopeless, meaningless world, and from somewhere I heard a victorious "Yes" in answer to my question of the existence of an ultimate purpose. At that moment, a light was lit in a distant farmhouse, which stood on the horizon as if painted there, in the midst of the miserable grey of a dawning morning in Bavaria. "Et lux in tenebris lucent"—and the light shineth in the darkness."[84]

Hope and faith are different. Hope is logical thought as it recognizes facts, and is a confident expectation and desire for something good to occur in the future. Faith is a blind resolution that no matter how the facts come out, a positive outcome will always prevail.

Hope is based on the uncertainty of events around us. Our faith isn't concerned with uncertainty—only the belief that God has devised a plan, so whatever the outcome is, it's for the better. No matter a situation's eventual outcome, faith requires us to have full confidence that it's for the best in our lives.

---

84 *Man's Search for Meaning", Viktor E. Franklm 1946*

Faith and hope are related. As one source puts it: Faith and hope are complimentary. Faith is grounded in the reality of the past; hope is looking to the reality of the future. Without faith, there is not hope, and without hope there is not true faith. Many people of different religions have faith and hope.

We have "'in the hope of eternal life, which God, who does not lie, promised before the beginning of time' (Titus 1:2)."[85]

Here's an example of the relationship between faith and hope:

As a child, my father told me we were going to a professional football game on Sunday. I believed we were going to the game, based on my father's word—my faith. Along with my faith in my father came immense joy—my hope. My trust in my father's promise is my faith; my excitement and delight are the expressions of my hope.

Many people who have faith are still depressed and unhappy. Often, it's because they don't have hope, to inspire and use their faith.

On the other hand, there are also people unhappy because they hope often, but have little faith to support their hope. We need faith and hope together to achieve the life we desire.

In her poem "Hope is the thing with feathers," Emily Dickinson writes:

85 *http://biblehub.com//internet/bible, New International Version/2011*

"It's Not Fair": How Can We Deal with Social Challenges in Today's Culture?

Hope is the thing with feathers –

That perches in the soul –

And sings the tune without the words –

And never stops – at all –

I've often wondered, how do we know if we have faith and hope? Only you know. They are spiritual, deep in our hearts and souls, and strengths we carry daily. We cannot turn our faith and hope on and off—either they exist within us, or they don't.

Hope is essential for our souls and hearts. Without hope we lose our feeling of self-worth and belief in our future. In fact, when we lose all hope, we lose all desire to live. Hope is our only choice! One person without faith and hope is one too many. What wonderful gifts they are in life. All we need to do is reach out and make them ours.

A few years ago, one of my freshman students told me she wanted to attend the US Naval Academy. I can't tell you how many freshmen have told me they want to be fighter pilots, attend one of our military academies, be a Navy Seal or Army Ranger. Only a handful have accomplished these goals.

This particular student developed goals in and out of the classroom. She was intelligent, personable, and driven. She always wore a smile and was moving forward. In her junior year, she realized that being a member of an athletic team would enhance her qualifications. Not having much of an athletic background, she signed up for the cross country and track teams. She worked hard and eventually was running competitively on very well-regarded teams.

Her senior year, I conducted her physical fitness test for the Naval Academy. She was unable to perform a regulation chin-up, which was required to pass. That same day, she bought a bar and mounted it in her bedroom. She worked on chin-ups daily. She retook the test a couple of months later, and up she went, chin over bar. I was in disbelief, but she wasn't. During that senior year, she was notified of her selection to the Academy. She has recently graduated.

Without a doubt, she had hope and faith. She had goals, believed in herself, and overcame difficult challenges. Her faith and hope will serve her well as a naval officer.

Today, we face challenging times. Let's remember that our past was difficult and know that our future will likely be too. It's not a unique world we live in, though with our own unique problems and obstacles. We never want to quit on life, even with all its negativity and despair, but use our hope to see the kind of world we want it to be. Yes, this can result with change.

My mother, a person of immense faith, more than once called me idealistic. She was right, though I still cling to my hope for change and a better world.

Franklin D. Roosevelt said, "We have always held to the hope, the belief, the conviction, that there is a better life, a better world, beyond the horizon." And further, "The only limit to our realization of tomorrow will be our doubts of today. Let us move forward with strong and active faith."[86] This is our charge to make a difference and advocate for change, wherever change is needed.

Violence and hate won't bring peace and happiness. We've experienced much hate and anger. Have we not learned from our history? Followers need leaders, and today's leaders are lacking. If action is needed, we must act peacefully, with hope and faith. We hope one day all of society will want a peaceful future, where each child can grow free, with equality.

Most people envision a good and peaceful society not only for themselves but for their children. However, we're being challenged and exposed to various types of fear and hate all over the world. Some of this fear is unpreventable, most is not.

The media has presented this to us around the clock. True news and fake news, drenched with politics, as discussed earlier. However, terrorism, nuclear arms capabilities, natural disasters, lack of trust in political leadership, indiscriminate surveillance on citizenry, immigration concerns, global climate change, crime in our country, are all real. They cause us to perceive the world as a more dangerous place to live.

The days of leaving house doors unlocked, children playing outside in the dark, and having neighborhood

---

86 *http://ranker.com//internet/The Best Franklin D. Roosevelt Quotes*

socials, knowing one another by name, are well in the past. Almost everyone, including elementary-age children (and regardless of a family's budget), have cell phones and other gadgets. The days of playing kick the can, whiffle ball, and hopscotch—that is, outdoor fun—are over.

A parent's own social anxiety of fear and mistrust results in this. It's sad. But we have no one to blame but ourselves, as we lock our doors, turn on the TV or our laptops, plug in our earphones, iPads and cells in hand. Family togetherness and communication has diminished. For many reasons, we truly believe this is the way we must live.

Our culture has changed. Over time, we've been transformed into a society of fear and distrust. We're bombarded with threatening anonymous phone calls, hacks on our personal identities, scrupulous mail, and for some, government surveillance. There are an unknown number of felons freed early, because state politicians decided they could no long afford to imprison them. There are illegal immigrants with criminal records housed in sanctuary cities, in violation of our Constitution.

Poverty in our nation continues, with one of five people in California alone living in poverty.[87] Poor people fear for their futures. The wealthy are fearful someone is going to take their money away from them. The poor look for a more equitable distribution of wealth; the wealthy argue that

---

87 http://politifact.com//internet/articles/Chris Nichols/TRUE: California has the nation's highest poverty rate, when factoring in cost – of living/012017

they earned their keep and already pay unfair taxes.

This occurs in many different society's and political systems, and if we want it changed, our political system must be changed, and/or individuals must adapt and change. Then again, we should also heed the saying, "Be careful what you wish for—you just might get it."

This isn't a culture most of us grew up in, and many pray with hope we can go back in history and start over, for the generations ahead of us. The truth is, there's no turning back. We're much better off accepting our life and the world we live in, without hate and fear, and being proactive change makers. We begin with faith and hope, and action.

Can you imagine the world and all its peoples with this same faith and hope, mixed with love? My mother was right about me being an idealist, though without hope and faith, what do we have? I've told myself God won't do this for us. If we're waiting for his justice to bail us out, our faith is misplaced. He gave us the tools and his love; the work is ours, and to date we have repeatedly failed.

Each man and woman, regardless of race, color, or creed, how poor or wealthy, is capable of faith, hope, and love. These extraordinary gifts were given to each of us, and all we need to do is use them, feel them, share them. Unfortunately, as imperfect as we are, many choose not to, a waste to mankind.

Today, there is suffering all over the world, and in our country. There are cries of hope in seemingly hopeless circumstances; there are faithful cries and prayers for our future existence. We see numerous problems, affecting all of us, go unresolved. We wonder, what is the international community doing? What are our political leaders doing? What is our religion doing?

Our challenges today aren't all political, although many take the easy way out and blame all our problems on politicians and the government. That's simply not so.

As mentioned earlier, problems are more apt to be resolved if we state the problem clearly and accurately, obtain information, communicate honestly with ALL appropriate people, and proceed with reality. Here is where we often fail before we get started, spinning like tops, and solving little. Communicating with ALL involved parties, respecting other's opinions and considering their recommendations is a key to leadership and facilitating problem solving.

Through mankind's constant suffering, we keep our faith and hope. The hope that one day we'll recognize that we have a universal mission, one that includes ALL of humanity. No human being is more important than another. That our land was given to us, and we have a duty and obligation to keep it just and peaceful. We're also given the capacity, if we have the will, to live together with equality, peace, and love. This hope seems unreal, but how would humanity know, we have never given it a chance.

Hope isn't a delusional optimism we resort to because

we cannot accept reality. People die. Friends leave us. Careers fail. Marriages end in divorce. Dreams fade into darkness. Families live in poverty. Natural disasters and accidents hurt us. Evil does exist. Fairness isn't always fair. Justice isn't always justice. But through it all, hope remains. Nevertheless, as a choice—our only choice.

First, with hope and faith, despite everything, we expect a better future. Also, our hope must include seeing reality and truth, not chasing illusions. We don't want to follow leaders who are doomsters, who are never happy people, have little faith and hope, and want others to join their sullen lives. Often, those in need, drifting, searching to belong, and without faith and hope, are most susceptible to negativity and pessimism. These relationships usually don't fare well.

We must be leaders or follow leaders, know what needs to be changed, and continue to resist wrongs. Positive change can only occur by being steadfast and tenacious, with continued hope.

Do we see signs of hope? Sure we do. More emphasis on human rights and equality around the world, increased awareness and tolerance of different religions, youth reinvigorated to their churches and religions, increased educational and occupational opportunities for women and people of color, a seeming determination worldwide to overcome the resentments of the past, to forgive and move forward, and the desire to re-engage –communication and dialogue with those we oppose or disagree with.

The following is a speech I recently presented to nearly 300 high school students, parents, teachers, school administrators, and board members. The ceremony was the students annual JROTC ball. My thought for inserting the speech is not because I view it as outstanding or necessarily unique, but as noted in the speech, I hoped the students would be interested, be forced to think for and about themselves, and that they would remember being together on that Saturday night in March 2018.

Good evening!

Thank you for having me tonight — it's great to back with you and my honor!

To our special guests,

Wonderful parents,

To you dedicated teachers,

And, you students, the reason we are here tonight!

Wish I could say thank — you for inviting me but apparently you did not! You did not get the memo! So next week please don't demonstrate, protest, or throw tomatoes at the instructors. My visit was a secret!

You may be wondering what retirees do, besides act retired. I'm substitute teaching kindergarten thru 8th grade!

Also, I'm also writing a book! How about that! The title: "It's Not Fair" How Can We Deal with Social Challenges in Today's Culture?

It's a novice first book – Something I have always wanted to do –

If you get an opportunity to read it, send me your thoughts. I promise to reply.

I would like to share a few of my thoughts tonight regarding you and the world you live in today.

In reminiscing, there have been so many lectures, speeches, even classes in my life time I have forgotten or have meant little to me. It's not that I was inattentive or had an attitudinal problem, there was apparently little purpose, learning, or relevance involved. And then, there is some learning I will never forget and instilled in me hope for the future.

My hope is you will do some personal thinking and remember a few of these words and thoughts... and that we were together tonight.

First, we must understand and accept the fact we have no control over many things that occur in our society. With this understanding, we always want to be mentally, socially, and physically balanced and healthy. "Everything in moderation" my mother often reminded me, "everything in moderation."

What we CAN control is our own world. One major aspect we can take charge of is OURSELVES.

Our world today is spinning out of control. Regardless of who one is, most agree our nation is more divided today than in any time since probably the Civil War. This is a shame, but the reality we live in. We have red and blue states, conservatives, liberals, socialists, right wings, left wings, hundreds of activist groups, generation differences, even friction between males and females. And no, it's not one person, one political party, one group of people, or one race to blame. Those who live with anger, hate, fear, and worse, will not help us unify our country.

America's division has been occurring for decades and involved all of us and it will take ALL of us together to reunite. What will it take to unite us ...? I don't know, but I have hope.

To compound this division that separates us today is a multitude of social issues, important issues, important to you. And because of our division "we the people" are unable to resolve these issues. We simply can't work together, listen to and respect each other, include one another — we are not communicating and compromising. People are becoming emotional and losing hope. These life skills are so basic we begin learning as children.

The issues range from racism, gender equality, immigration, and interpreting the constitution and our laws. For instance, what are our rights today? What should they be? Why is there so much disagreement regarding our laws? Has it become acceptable today to break laws we don't believe in rather than to pursue changing an unpopular law?

Each issue raises many questions and they are tough and challenging. Much more difficult than often portrayed by the media, or on late night TV, twitter, Facebook, and Instagram.

Many Americans are questioning our judicial system and local and federal law enforcement agencies. We seemed confused regarding women's rights, the poverty in America today and how to fix it, our role and relationship with other countries, and agreement on the best ways to allocate our spending while at the same time balancing our nation's budget. These are only a few of the pressing issues.

Let's look at an example: When writing my book, I wondered if poverty in America was a social justice issue? In a documented 2017 report of most popular American social issues, poverty was not addressed. It's as if, Americans realize poverty exists, however rationalize it as is inevitable and unsolvable. It's just too dog gone hard!

What I learned and what Americans may not know, is the extent of poverty, and the actions being taken or not, to decrease it.

What is startling are the statistics. According the US Census Bureau using household income, our nations poverty rate in 2016 was 12.7 percent, with 40.6 million people in poverty. The total population of the US was 319.9 million. The number of people without health insurance in 2016 was 28.1 million people. The estimated number of homeless Americans in 2017 rose to 554,000.

These poverty rates have been similar over the past 30 years. However, the child poverty rate in 2016 increased to 18.5 million therefore, one in five children are living in poverty today. This is a tragedy – children are so helpless to do anything regarding their living conditions. "Where have I been," I thought while writing. And, what are we doing to address the 40 million people who continue to live in poverty? In researching this issue, it is apparent three things can prevent people from slipping into poverty; having a full-time job, obtaining at least a high school degree, and accomplishing family planning. Many of our poor have none of these, and few have all.

I wrote in my book, "The Story of Joe, The Barber." Unfortunately, I do not have time to read it to you, I don't want to cut into your dance time!

The story portrays an immigrant family from Italy with literally nothing but what they could carry on their backs and eventually rising from poverty. Starting a barber business with a mere room and two chairs, Joe's family worked hard to overcome the adversity of being poor. With some good fortune they helped another poor family escape poverty and pursue their family dreams. Both their children went on to graduate college.

Attempting to defeat poverty does not always end with these results. Hopefully, the story strengthens our faith and love, and rekindles our hope for all mankind.

This issue of poverty is one of many we need to deal with if we want to continue as a world leader. America's leadership should never be used as boastful or pumping our chests, or to infer we are superior. What it means, or SHOULD mean, is being a humble role model for human rights and equality for All people in All nations. It means we should assist others less fortunate that they may have lasting peace, safety, and the opportunity for happiness. And we should continue to aid those countries in need, when we have the will, resources, and the ability to do so. Some people will argue with me over this last point. Even my mother has called me idealistic with some humor. I have always laughed and told her we'll wait one day and see!

Unfortunately, today is not the day, as we struggle to uphold the leadership responsibility the world expects of us. To set any example, and you all know this, one must be the example. In a nation divided, we have so much hate, anxiety, and uncertainty, our emotions often run deep as there seems a tremendous tension in the air surrounding us. We are stagnated and in a stalemate. However, our nation will move again in a positive direction, I'm hopeful and know it to be!

It is difficult to say or feel, but today we are not in a position to lead others. Our nation's focus today must be in our own house and back yard. Your focus should not be on what YOU cannot control, but on what YOU can, your life, yourself.

Now, let's look at you. No one in the world is exactly like you! You upper classmen have heard me discuss this in class when we learned our personalities. You are unique, one of a kind, your mind, heart, soul, your love to give, and talents to share with the world.

Take a moment occasionally to reflect on this fact, Me, Myself, and I, in a world I DO CONTROL and am free to navigate through. However, let's be clear your self- reflection of your own thoughts, values, and daily growth, DOES NOT separate you from the outer world, or should it. What your self-analysis DOES is make you a stronger more engaging person and productive member in society. By controlling your own world, you can be a positive influence for others and MAKE A DIFFERENCE in the world around you! No doubt about it!

Keep in mind, as you reflect, on all the beauty and good in the world around you. Don't take for granted but cherish the many things you are grateful for, the good and loving people in your life, your hopes and dreams, and what brings you happiness.

At the same time, you will see all the things people are not — the same things you can be. Each of us may see these things differently yet all of us have a choice of WHO we want to be.

When I discussed earlier unresolved issues affecting millions of Americans there are underlying reasons for our division, for what is separating us, and our inability to solve problems. You may have your opinions: Maybe to you it's a lack of patriotism and loyalty; or unethical behavior and values, people's loss of hope and love; a reluctance to communicate and listen to each other, leaders lacking leadership and integrity, apathy or the "me" attitude, ... or whatever your thoughts may be. The importance here is what YOU see and feel the world is NOT, is what you CAN BE.

And although no one can tell you what to do in life, what to believe in or say, or the kind of person you should be, there are basic human behavioral traits we should all adhere to. A few are: being honest and trustworthy; treating ALL people with dignity and respect; being compassionate and helping those in need; and having a value system that is nonnegotiable.

Unfortunately, not all mankind meets these basics even though we each have a choice in our

Me, myself, and I world.

You have control of the kind of person you want to be, and no one can take it away from you. I caution you though, it can often be easier to go with the trendy and popular than to think for yourself, listen and consider the voices of others, and make your own decisions. You always want to hold on to the real you, your hopes and dreams. Remember there is no one like you – never let go of Me, Myself and I.

I conclude with these thoughts for you:

- As you continue to grow, I hope you will receive challenging or bias education, so you will be forced to think critically and FOR YOURSELF.
- I hope you see and feel the victims pain of bullying and abuse so that you may become more compassionate and tolerant for all people regardless of who they are, their social status or popularity.
- I hope you lose your social media privileges for an extended time so that you can experience and enjoy more of the wonderful world around you.
- And yes, I hope each of you get an opportunity to LEAD and then experience failure and understand that great leaders often fail and always persevere. You and I are no exceptions.

- I wish some drama in your lives and you will have just enough pain to take control of yourself with self-esteem and strength to live without it.
- Lastly, you'll be confronted with many ethical and moral decisions challenging your values and CHARACTER and the real you.

I hope you see the need to often be challenged in life ... to understand the lesson. So often we are told what the lesson or message is, but we must experience and learn for ourselves.

Never quit on your hope for the real you!

Always Remember ... You have a unique gift to offer this world. Whether it is with your hands, your mind or with your heart, share Yourself with others.

Be true to yourself, be kind to yourself, and respect the uniqueness of those around you. When you do, you will be giving this world an amazing gift ...YOU!

Thank you once again for having me. I hope you remember being together this evening in JOY and happiness.

It seems as though we're always starting over, learning, making mistakes, and relearning. But what choice do we have? What choice do my young students have? And, what choice did a young girl from North Korea have?

One North Korean defector, Yeonmi Park, shared her story at the 2017 Global Teen Leaders at the Just Peace Summit. "To you, he was a joke. To me, he [Kim Jong Un] was a God."

During her presentation, she spoke of public executions performed arbitrarily, whole families sent to Korean work camps, surviving on "grasshoppers and dragonflies" and forced to watch her mother raped. It was a harrowing portrayal of life in the secretive communist nation. For Yeonmi each day was a nightmare, yet it was reality. However, she also shared her hope, which in part stems from her "rediscovered faith in humanity."[88] Most of us may wonder how she could rediscover her faith during all this adversity and pain. Her faith and hope kept this courageous young lady moving forward. She always remained hopeful, ready, and patient in life, somehow knowing her opportunity would come.

Yeonmi talks of her hope to one day go home and be with nature. She loves her country and its people, just not its leadership. She wants her people freed.

I've thought about this a long time, and I believe she's right—until the North Korean people understand their reality and see the new world around them, there will be no change. We must find ways to bring this world to them, and for the first time provide the opportunity of hope in their lives.

---

88 *http://huffingtonpost.com//internet/articles/Nadya Okamoto/The Story of a North Korean Defector/03112017*

As the international community decides how to handle North Korean leadership, we must not forget the millions like Yeonmi Park, who are imprisoned, used as slaves, brainwashed, and worse.

The world is cautiously watching North Korea and its nuclear buildup. In all I've read and seen, there is little discussion regarding the North Korean people themselves. The population of North Korea is 25,428,246, and should be an important consideration in any action taken on the Korean peninsula. One could compare North Korea today to North Vietnam in the 1960s to 1970s: a relatively small number of communist dictators and tyrants using fear to rule and manipulate the hearts and minds of millions of innocent civilians.

The Korean War ended almost 70 years ago. Seeing North Korea's present state, one might ask: Should we have continued in North Korea and forced the communists to surrender? Were the risks, peace and liberty for the North Korean people worth the rewards? In answering these questions, consider a just Korea. Also, consider the millions of North Koreans, like Yeonmi, unable to live freely.

Nearly 70 years later, little change has occurred for generations of North Koreans. Where is the hue and cry? Does anyone care? Or are the millions of people in North Korea not worth the international community's concern? Is Korea now important only because of its nuclear capability? What responsibility do the US or other countries have to assist people in need around the world? Many in the US, with their individual needs and wants, would say, "None— it's not our business." I disagree.

The US can't be involved everywhere in the world where there is suffering. We don't have the manpower, budget, or public support, and therefore must prioritize our strategic interests and security.

I feel alone, though know I'm not, regarding the millions of North Korean citizens and their lives without justice and hope. How can they have faith and hope when they don't know who and what they are?

North Korea remains one the most repressive, authoritarian nations in the world. Over the decades their dictatorship continues to generate fearful obedience by using public executions, arbitrary detention, and forced labor; tightening travel restrictions to prevent North Koreans from escaping; and systematically persecuting those with religious contacts inside and outside the country.

There's little freedom of expression, religion, and access to information. Therefore, few know the world around them; they're brainwashed from early childhood. There's inhumane treatment in detention, including children facing deplorable conditions, slavery, sexual abuse, beatings by guards, and possible execution. The government uses forced labor to control its people and sustain its economy. The people have no rights regarding their labor. The people work when and where they are told.

The North Korean justice system uses the death penalty, often without judicial due process, and is administered for a wide variety of political and common crimes. Personnel in the criminal justice system have wide discretion and are allegedly authorized to operate without regard to Koreans' formal legal rights. Few trials exist, and most inmates are sent to prison camps without them.

Information regarding North Korea is difficult to obtain. However, according to a January 2016 article in *The Guardian*, UNICEF declared that "about 25,000 children in North Korea require immediate treatment for malnutrition after a drought cut food production by a fifth and the government reduced rations." North Korean children face many problems. At least 40% of the people live below the poverty line. Most workers earn $2 to $3 per month.

Poverty is at a critical level and periodically worsens because of natural disasters and international sanctions. Many children find themselves homeless and facing adverse living conditions. And the food crisis has resulted in thousands of deaths.[89]

It's time the international community takes necessary actions to affect change in North Korea. This action shouldn't be centered around politics, but on basic humanitarian, health, and justice concerns. Over the past years, there have been idle words and idle hands, and little change.

---

89 *http://borgenproject.org//internet/TheBlog/Marcelo Guadiana/10 Facts About Poverty in North Korea/16102016*

The options for change and an action plan for North Korea need to be examined realistically:

- War isn't a practical option. Experts predict millions of causalities in the event of war. Seoul, Korea, alone has a municipal population of 24.1 million people, and Tokyo, Japan, has 37.9 million people. Seoul is 35 miles from the North Korean border, and could be badly damaged by North Korean artillery. According to a new report from the 38 North, a North Korea analysis group based at Johns Hopkins University's U.S. – Korea Institute, "casualties would be catastrophic, including 7.7 million injuries; and casualties could reach as high as 3.8 million in both Tokyo and Seoul." North Korea itself would likely be annihilated.[90]

- Continued sanctions haven't prevented or slowed North Korea's will to develop nuclear arms, with the ability to deploy them worldwide. North Korea has shown they have "workarounds" to sanctions. Their leadership isn't overly concerned about their people's welfare; therefore, sanctions primarily impact the citizenry.

- Projecting military deterrence–that is, a show of force–is an oft-used solution that needs to continue.

---

90 http://time.com// internet/articles/Eli Meixler/Here's How Deadly a North Korea Nuclear Attack Could Be/10062017

- Diplomacy—communication leading to resolution—is the best solution. However, North Korean leaders are unwilling to negotiate. They have gone too far and believe they must have nuclear capability to survive. China is a key participant in any possible diplomatic matters but is reluctant to take further actions, as it's concerned about its own national interests.

- Leadership change would be a good option, if such change was initiated by the North Korean people. However, this scenario is very different than other historical revolutions worldwide, because the people live in fear, are brainwashed, and have little knowledge of the outside world. Therefore, this is unlikely to occur.

The United Nations is now confronted with a serious dilemma. North Korea's weapons program is a grave threat to the Asia-Pacific region and the entire international community. It's wise to continue diplomacy, with increased sanctions and a show of force, and for the United Nations— specifically, South Korea, Japan, China, Russia, and the US—to be prepared militarily.

What's concerning is the potential for a worldwide nuclear buildup to counter the North Koreans. It wouldn't be prudent for the Asian region to take this approach, nor the US to increase its nuclear arsenal beyond current arms control agreements. Few nations in the world would favor a reversion to a nuclear arms race. Rather than restore nuclear arms, North Korea needs to be shut down. Together, many Americans and people throughout the world have this hope.

In summary, and at time of this writing, Kim Jong-un has agreed to a US–North Korea Summit. Kim Jong-un has recently announced he will suspend nuclear and long-range missile tests. He has also offered to discuss "denuclearization" and the possibility of peace on the Korean peninsula. There is reason for optimism and hope, however, if these negotiations begin, they will take time.

It's time to completely isolate North Korea. To do so will require all nations to support freezing all assets to North Korea. China is North Korea's main trading partner and the most important country able to exert leverage on the rogue regime. We can only hope this will occur.

If continuing sanctions and diplomacy are ineffective, two options remain: to live with North Korea as a nuclear power, or to use military means to topple the North Korean regime. No other scenarios exist.

My hope is North Korea will disarm, Korea will be reunited as a free society, and its very repressed people liberated.

We're fortunate to be US citizens and live in such a strong country. With this strength, we at times must lead in assisting and aiding people in need. It's our moral responsibility to humanity.

Being fortunate, we have the freedom to teach hope

to our youth, not on a whiteboard, but by being positive, caring role models. We motivate and bolster up children. We increase their self-esteem. We ensure that they reach every ounce of their potential, using their God-given abilities. We provide children with the stimulation and opportunities in life to be hopeful. We give them our faith, so they may cherish their hope for a lifetime.

I recently met Jeanette Beck, a 98-year-old mother of three from Phoenix, Oregon. She's an amazing woman, with the mind of a woman much younger, a gentle smile, and a willingness to talk with anyone and everyone. Without hesitation, she agreed to sit with me and chat. So we had coffee at her daughter's home.

Ms. Beck has always felt that life is unfair, and according to her, "We take what is handed to us and do our best." She stated, "People of all ages use the words 'it's not fair,' because they don't realize and think about it." As an example of unfairness, she mentioned soldiers who are continually deployed around the globe. The soldiers go regardless of the hows or whys.

In a positive tone, she discussed how our country has changed during her lifetime: "We never locked our doors. People trusted each other and helped one another, and this has changed." She also stated, "There is a steady decline in loyalty to our country," and mentioned that much of what happens today revolves around "the almighty dollar."

Ms. Beck seemed very aware of current events.

She related her childhood, growing up with no technology, not even a radio. There were ten children in the family, with kerosene lights, an old chimney, outdoor toilets, and no refrigerator. When her brother was 13 years old, he started working in a mill and bought the family its first refrigerator. Jeanette was the oldest child, and I was waiting to hear about her responsibilities and challenges in the home. She never spoke about them. I wasn't surprised. I immediately assumed Ms. Beck, unlike those from younger generations, simply accepted her responsibilities and family expectations as a "given." Likely she performed as big sister with the same smile and attitude she has today.

When I asked her about the importance of faith, her eyes lit up. Faith is what seems to keep her bright, optimistic, and happy. Her comments were that she "always had something to look forward to, and belief in God was her faith," and "if we did not have faith, we just live and die." She believes, "Lots of people have faith, and lots don't."

Jeanette feels that people can have faith and not be weekly churchgoers and can certainly feel free to question their religion. She said, "If you don't ask questions, you don't grow. When I would question my mother regarding God and his fairness, she would say, 'Didn't you ever think he would say no?'"

She feels hope is important to a person's life. It's like having a dream. And she mentioned the song "You Gotta Have Hope." Jeanette used the example of immigrants hoping for a better life and said she wished their path to citizenship were easier. She's concerned about children who have been illegally brought into the US, who have lived here and may now be deported. I assured her that this won't happen (although in hindsight, I probably shouldn't have provided this assurance).

She's obviously a lady of strong faith and lasting hope, with a purpose in this world. I wish I'd known her for a lifetime ... her gentle tranquility and wisdom is inspiring.

The words in "You Gotta Have Hope" of hope and dreams, of peace and love, and of letting God in our lives is the essence of who Ms. Beck is.

To be effective parents for our children we must have hope. Then as parents we instill this same hope into our children.

Once a child is blessed with the foundation of hope in their lives, they cherish it. Their faith and desire for prayer is a simple way for a teen to sustain hope. A following prayer for young adults to be used any time, any place, anywhere:

A Teen's Daily Prayer

Hi, God, it's always nice to talk with you

Give me the strength today to be the best person I can be

Your word and touch, so I may continue moving forward

Your belief in me, so I can believe in others

Your love for me, so I can love myself and others

Your plans for me that inspire my daily hope

Stay with me today and every day—I need you

Thank you, God, for letting me be me, with my faith and humility

Lastly, I ask that if I stumble or fail, you are by my side

Helping me up as you always have. Amen.

—Gene Matera

CHAPTER EIGHT

"The Greatest of These Is Love"

"And now these three remain: faith, hope,
and love. But the greatest of these is love."
—1 Corinthians 13:13

I can't help wondering why there's such intense negativity in the world, when there's also so much overwhelming love. Do we need hurt, pain, and hatred for our very existence? Or is it possible one day for all mankind to live together in peace, with love? Imagine if we spent more time acting on our love rather than on what separates us. Imagine.

Beginning this final chapter, I told myself, "You're not an expert on love." But who is? Surely many are more knowledgeable on the subject, are more experienced, and are loved more. Yet, having been married for 31 years, provided some necessary welcomed confidence. With my faith and hope, I continued.

Based on societal norms at the time, I married late in life. In my late 20s, I began asking myself questions regarding marriage, love, and why some people married at early ages and others much later. More and more people began asking me questions. One thing I did know: love would appear when I chose it, and I would know when. This idea was consoling to me, myself, and I.

Love is the most powerful emotion we can experience. Most of us believe we know the true meaning of love, yet often become confused about it. Love has many different meanings. What we do know is that love expresses a human virtue based on compassion, affection, and kindness—it's our state of being.

The ancient Greek used seven words to define the different types of love:

Storage: natural affection, the love you share with your family.

Philia: the love that you have for friends.

Eros: sexual and erotic desire kind of love (positive or negative).

Agape: this is the unconditional love, or divine love.

Ludus: this is the playful love, like childish love or flirting.

Pragma: long standing love. The love in a married couple.

Philautia: the love of the self (negative or positive)."[91]

We feel different emotions for different situations and people. Regardless of our emotional state and feelings, we use the same word: love. We can say we love different people, and mean it, but actually have different feelings for each of them. So who and what we love can be confusing.

We often use the word *love* incorrectly, when it's unemotional and without feeling toward other people. A couple of examples are: I love Italian food, or I love your idea. We can change this by substituting more appropriate words for love: Italian is my favorite food, or your idea is excellent.

If people overuse the word, they diminish their feeling of real love. On the other hand, if people rarely use it, they may be incapable of showing their emotions and feelings, depriving themselves of experiencing love. We can never use it enough with the people we truly love.

With love, you get out what you put into it. First, we learn how to feel and cultivate our love and know the different situations/types of love. Then, how to recognize the situations when we are feeling them. And, lastly, we share our love with others.

91 http://unisoultheory.com//internet/articles/Robyn Reisch/The Ancient Greeks Recognized 7 Types of Love – Which Defines You?/02022017

Falling in love with someone is easy. The challenge is remaining in love. If one has difficulty sustaining love in a relationship, it isn't love. Love is always beautiful. If it isn't, it's not love. This is a good reason to take your time and experience different situations and feelings with people before determining your love. Therefore, love is as much a learned skill as it is an emotion. In doing so, we determine whether we're really in love or not.

Here are a few things I've learned about love over the years:

- Love cannot be manufactured; it cannot be turned on and off. And all humans, the strongest and weakest, can love and be loved.
- Love can hurt more than anything else we experience in life. Without loving we can never be happy.
- Love is beautiful when we're willing to give all of ourselves—physically, mentally, and spiritually. We have true love when we're consciously willing to sacrifice ourselves to our partner. Anything less, and love dies.

Committing to love is a lot to ask of a person. The demands of falling in love, being in love, and then sustaining love are great, encompassing myriad emotions and feelings. Often, the work and commitment necessary for everlasting love is overwhelming, and no longer emotionally and physically achievable. When this occurs, love falters.

Once the "honeymoon" period ends, real love begins. For many people this can be a highly emotional and confusing time. So many things change during a relationship that it can cause us to question why our love today doesn't feel similar to our wedding day. The routines and stability of everyday life take over and bring reality to marriage. Our love can be challenged.

I often wonder during a wedding, with all the excitement, joy, and family and friends, if grooms and brides have deeply considered the vows and their meaning prior to saying "I do." We'll never know, and that's good reason as to why premarital counseling is important. Maybe counseling should become mandatory before marriage.

Perhaps this lack of deep consideration of the commitment being made contributes to failed marriages: "about 40 to 50 percent of married couples in the US divorce. The divorce rate for subsequent marriages is even higher."[92] This rate has existed in the US since the late 1970s.[93]

In nearly every exchange of vows, the word *love* is used, and the responsibility of each member to ensure this love is eternal.

An example of a vow, and of course there are many:

GROOM, repeat after me:

_____ BRIDE, as your husband,

92 https://www.nytimes.com/2014/12/02/upshot/the-divorce-surge-is-over-but-the-myth-lives-on.html
93 http://time.com/4575495/divorce-rate-nearly-40-year-low/

I promise to care for you,

trust your LOVE,

be responsive to your needs,

communicate my feelings,

and behave in a way that shows my LOVE and respect,

I will do these things because I LOVE you

And want to live out each day of my life with you.

BRIDE, repeat after me: (The same words as above)

We shouldn't consider divorce a failure, but rather a life experience to build on and move forward. We're always learning about ourselves and others, and love provides us this opportunity.

Furthermore, we cannot predict when love will begin, how long it will last, and why it may end, if it ever does end. Love should never be taken for granted; it isn't a lifetime guarantee.

When one finds love, hold onto it. When one loses love, walk away from it. In the long run, this is the healthy reaction. However, before walking away, make every effort and take every opportunity to rekindle the love you once felt. Conversely, staying in an unhappy relationship for the wrong reasons will only result in continued hurt and emotional pain.

Likewise, our children need our unconditional love. They need to know that if we make promises, we follow through. From their birth we make a commitment to their lives, their friends and daily activities, ball games, and school functions. We're there for them, wherever that may be, and ensure they are valued and respected members of the family. We communicate with our children and show them we're interested and care about their intellectual, physical, and social growth. This means we demonstrate the importance of education in the family, as well as our children's faith, morality, and values.

As parents we need to show our love for our children, as well as our love for each other. Children are perceptive and observant, usually adopting their parents' behaviors and values. Therefore, parents' relationships with their children and themselves is extremely important to their children's growth and ability to love and feel loved.

Quite often, this requires parents to make personal changes to improve their behavior and commitment. Both parents must be willing and able to work together in their marriage, as well as in their parenting. To do so, parents must have faith and the desire to love one another, regardless of trivial daily challenges and personal needs and wants.

In doing so, we demonstrate our love to our children in the hope that they'll emulate it in their lives. We must never forget that our children are always watching and learning from us.

Parents are the first two people who teach children what love is, and our children rely on our example to show that love is real. We want our children to know love is healthy, safe, and beautiful.

We want them to grow up believing in their hearts what Alfred Lord Tennyson once wrote:

"I hold it true, whate'er befall;

I feel it when I sorrow most;

'Tis better to have loved and lost

Than never to have loved at all."[94]

I've known a couple in our neighborhood for many years; they have three children very close in age. The couple are ordinary people—they work hard, are good friends and citizens.

For some 20 years they have dedicated their life together to supporting and guiding their children. All three children were heavily involved in athletics, school activities, and church obligations. They began their athletic careers at early ages, seeming to play year around. They were always coming and going, seven days a week, 12 months a year.

What was somewhat unique about the couple is that they attended all their children's activities and sports events. I thought, "What are they missing in life? Personal time, time for their own interests, vacations, travel?" I thought

94 http://goodreads.com//internet/quotes/Alfred Tennyson

about the commitment these two made to their children and how it seemed to bind their family together. I thought about how they never complained regarding their roles in life or showed anything but joy and love for their children. Their family was always together.

After years of observing this couple, I realized their purpose and passion in life was their love for their children. Their children's welfare and happiness was their priority. I saw how this couple's love inspired their children to reciprocate their happiness to their parents and others.

The children are grown now and have moved away. Now in their twenties, two children are happily married, I'm told. All the children have college degrees. Two are teachers, and the other works in marketing and is a college coach.

And I pondered further, thinking that like so many things in life, you get out what you put into it. The love for our children is worth our hard work and effort. My hope is that most parents provide such love.

In 1986, while visiting my family while on leave from the Air Force, I met my wife. She was a nurse with my mother at a hospital for the developmentally disabled. Having no key for the family home, I visited my mother at work.

Six months later we were married, and in the same year departed for a military assignment to Zaragoza, Spain. For the next three years we lived in a mountain home, with no telephone capability.

My wife's family was in shock, although they remained silent. I still imagine what they were thinking: "What is this stranger doing, taking our daughter from a small Wisconsin community to Europe for the next three years? What is he thinking? Or is he thinking?"

I was ready and prepared for marriage, but had no thoughts of having children. It simply hadn't crossed mind. I still had a desire to travel, see the world, and remain committed to my career. My wife also enjoyed traveling and supported my career, though she wanted to start a family. Two years later, the first of our three girls was born in Spain.

Neither my wife nor I spoke Spanish. Today we still joke that the Air Force assigned us to Spain because they thought *Matera* was Spanish, and I therefore knew the language. To my memory, no one ever asked if either of us knew Spanish.

The Spanish doctor didn't speak English, nor did anyone else in the medical facility our daughter was born in. The doctor was middle-aged man, personable, and seemed competent. My wife liked him. What else did we have to go on? Our other option to resolve the language barrier was to travel to Madrid, some 170 miles away. We agreed to stay in Zaragoza.

The pregnancy and realization that we were having a baby drew us closer. More self-centered than my wife, I realized I needed to make some changes in my life. Both of us now knew we would need to balance the lust to live a couple's life with raising and loving a newborn. The responsibility of being a father and husband was upon me sooner than I'd imagined.

My uncertainty about fatherhood, coupled with my wife's anxiety about having a child in a foreign country with little communication, also bonded us. We were in this together. We gave each other confidence and hope, and our love grew stronger.

One night while watching a horror movie (a poor choice) I said, "It's time to go." Barely able to get my wife into the car, off we drove in silence under the moonlit sky, down the endless mountain road to the hospital. The 15 miles seemed like 50. Just keep the car on the road, I told myself.

We arrived in time for my wife to be prepped for delivery. In Spanish, they told me to wait in the outer room. In muy malo español, I asked why I wasn't allowed in delivery. The doctor indicated it was customary for the father to wait in the outer room. My wife, in better Spanish, responded that we were unaware of this custom, and she would like me there.

Away they rolled her. I remained in the outer room, feigning a lack of understanding. The doctor, somewhat confused and agitated, threw a smock at me and mumbled, walking away. I observed the birth of our first child, the birth of life I will never forget.

As it turned out, our beautiful newborn traveled

everywhere with us on my back, always talking and pulling. I sang, she kicked.

During the Christmas holiday, two months after her birth, the three of us huddled by our tree. I told my daughter I would always love her. I would always be there for her and give her 100% of myself, and I would ensure her every opportunity to be the kind of person she wants to be.

I looked down at her in my arms, in the light of the tree, and she was smiling up at me, with her big eyes and cheeks. I held her like she was a multimillion-dollar Rembrandt—so tiny, fragile, and beautiful. I knew then that the changes in my life were a blessing.

Throughout the years, as imperfect as my wife and I were, we held onto a few basic values:

- We sustained and showed our love for each other.
- We maintained our faith and provided the girls with the opportunity to pursue their chosen faith.
- We gave the girls hope, and a variety of opportunities and experiences, so they could become strong, responsible, and independent adults and make their own decisions in life.
- And lastly, we treated others with respect, dignity, and compassion. This love for others has benefitted our daughters.

Gandhi once said, As capable as we are of loving individuals, we can also love groups of people. An example, and relevant to fairness and justice in our society, is our love of country.

I love my country—always have and always will. I consider myself patriotic, which shouldn't be misconstrued as having any political connotation.

As mentioned earlier, with real love comes heartfelt emotions and feelings. And feelings and emotions often result in disagreement and debate. Many love and accept our country for what it is, with hope for a better future, and others love but feel the need to disagree or speak out to initiate perceived change. An example of the latter is someone who loves the US, but criticizes US foreign policy matters or immigration laws and initiatives. America needs both these groups of people.

My love of country is rooted in our history, the courageous work, persistence, and sacrifice of a few to provide American ideals I believe in. I'm fortunate to be living in a democratic country with values of freedom, individual and human rights, and the opportunity for all citizens to pursue happiness.

I have come to a time in my life, when observing a minority of people who profess "hate" for or "embarrassment" of America, to simply let it go. This realization doesn't diminish my daily sorrow and disappointment. My belief is that you can't love your country without being proud of it and its accomplishments. This is true of all citizens in all countries. When people in any walk of life are unwilling to be positive catalysts, we need to move forward without them.

My question to these people, without emotion and nonjudgmental, would be, "Do you really know America?"

No one needs to defend our country; our accomplishments speak for themselves.

Do the self-professed "America haters" realize that, according to the Congressional Research Service (CRS), the US provided nearly $49 billion of foreign aid in 2015?[95] Are they aware of the Marshall Plan, a US initiative, which provided over $13 billion to finance Europe's economic recovery after World War II? That the US has repeatedly been the most generous country in the world, promoting economic development and welfare across the globe?

According to *Forbes*, in 2012 the US provided economic aid to 184 countries and military aid to 142 countries. The US provides this assistance to help countries remain stable, secure, and peaceful. Yes, the US benefits from having a stable, peaceful world, as do all countries and peoples.

Who do we aid and why?

- The US provides aide to our allies in need.
- We aid countries susceptible to overthrow by dictatorships and tyrants.
- We aid the international community and countries fighting terrorism.

---

95 *http://fas.org//internet/CongressionalResearch Service/Tarnoff and Lawson/Foreign Aid: An Introduction to U.S. Programs/06172016*

- We continually provide aid and manpower for humanitarian relief efforts, to respond to acute disasters, poverty reduction, healthcare, and other development programs around the world.
- We provide ongoing funding to some of the world's poorest countries.

The US provides more aid to more countries than any other country in the world. It has been estimated that with US aid, millions of lives have been saved. Bill Gates stated that medical interventions such as anti-polio and anti-HIV/AIDS and polio campaigns have a tremendous global impact, especially on poor countries, bolstering both economies and political stability.[96]

Along with monetary aid, thousands of American physicians, engineers, teachers, military and law enforcement personnel, State Department officials, have provided assistance, many volunteering to assist the poor and needy. Rarely is this front page news, and most of us don't know what these men and women have accomplished, but they selflessly serve others. Often their commitment has little to do with American political interests, and much to do with others' welfare.

These Americans help build schools, provide education for children, prevent diseases and administer medicine, build infrastructure and technology, train and educate, etc. Many countries they visit are high-risk and dangerous

96 http://time.com/4704550/bill-gates-cutting-foreign-aid-makes-america-less-safe/

environments.

They come and go, without fanfare or acknowledgement. They do it because they love their country and believe they are making a difference in less fortunate nations.

No American needs to apologize for America.

In the early 1990s, while I was a young officer serving in the Pentagon, our boss visited a group of us on the job. He wanted a volunteer over Christmas to escort a US congressman on a mission to Vietnam. The room went dead silent, and heads went down. I remember hating the silence and said, "I'll go."

Later that day I received my instructions. To my surprise the congressman and I would transport, on military aircraft, half a million dollars' worth of pharmaceutical supplies, drop the pallet over Vietnam, land, meet with Vietnamese officials, and the next day return home. I remember thinking that I didn't realize our country did these sorts of things.

I still wonder about the many unknown and daily humanitarian accomplishments of American men and women throughout the world. We don't need to be informed— true service doesn't require it. Rather than be ashamed or apologize, we should be proud and remain humble.

As with my visit to Vietnam, I traveled to many countries, and I often told my students that the first thing I met when deboarding the aircraft in many countries was a soldier with a weapon staring at me. That's not to say my stay was unpleasant, or the people were unfriendly, or I didn't enjoy the many cultures. But after weeks and often months in foreign lands, I always looked forward to coming home.

No country I have lived in or visited provides their citizenry the freedoms and opportunities we have in America. It's our national belief to be inclusive and provide equal opportunity to all citizens. Occasionally, we stumble and fail. In the end, however, it's always the individual's decision about what to do with their freedom and opportunity.

My love for country doesn't blind me to the fact that we have shortcomings and challenges ahead. In the past decade or so, our country hasn't been unified, disagreeing on what needs to change, and therefore unable to implement change.

I have faith that the vast majority of Americans love their country. However, our love for country can differ, depending on our cultural backgrounds, individual and group interests, and attitudes. Only by understanding and accepting our differences can we unite to correct and learn from our failures and develop progressive change.

Also, I get reenergized because of my belief in the importance of love. With faith and hope, love is a blessing. It should be the foundation of everything we do.

Often my students and I would discuss how they want to be remembered by their classmates and friends, after completing school. And then, how they want to be remembered in old age, reflecting back on their lives. I have intentionally been a listener at the whiteboard, recording the student's comments.

Every year the students responded similarly. Being teens, some humor generally began the discussion. Once we settled, the room was always quiet. The students were thinking, and no one wanted to be the initiator. Then a voice, then two, and soon many students were participating.

I pretty much knew what I'd be writing on the whiteboard.

I have kept this class assignment on my cell. The student responses included, "being a nice person," "good morals," "a good friend," "someone who constantly helped others and served," "a person with a good attitude and humorous," "a leader," "a caring person" "a person who loved life and always smiled," "a good citizen," "keeping strong relationships and a happy marriage," and the list continued. Many of the responses were repeated. They were heartfelt; they were sincere.

Over the years, with hundreds of students participating, it was evident that they wanted to be remembered for the kind of person they were, and their care and compassion for others, rather than personal achievement, popularity, success, or status. Although teens will rarely discuss "love" in an open forum, this was the implication: they wanted to love and be loved.

After our classroom discussion, I asked the students to consider themselves in old age and write a short story regarding their life from early childhood through the elder years. They would need to think about the person they want to be and their goals and dreams for life.

Remarkably, it was one assignment all students completed and enjoyed. Many students asked to share their papers with the class. Once again, the virtue of "loving others" was a dominant theme. Many still had their papers upon graduation and asked me to sign them.

If teens feel this way, what is it that occurs in many adult lives to prevent them from experiencing and demonstrating their desired love?

Preteens obviously are different. They "love" everyone or no one depending on the hour and day. They too live in the same great big world, but only see the smallest of images; their family, friends, schools, and social activities, church, etc. They have little understanding of true love, nor does society expect them to. Their lives rotate on being accepted, "finding themselves", and making it through the day hopefully with some fun and accomplishment, and not in the principal's office. A pat on the back, recognition, and some reward or award certainly helps their attitude and motivation. Love is a funny term to them and yet there is a wonderment in their eyes. Their relationships with one another are building blocks to learning what love is. As adults, we need to seize this opportunity to nurture this need and desire.

A few weeks ago, while substitute teaching for a 7th grade class I met the primary teacher before school for the daily lesson plans, summary of students, and further instructions. As we were talking I noticed a large piece of paper on a wall with words "SOCIAL CONTRACTS" with words underneath it. I asked the teacher if she would explain this. She stated it was started this year. The students periodically develop behaviors they want in their classroom. They then decide during the week what students/the class itself demonstrate these expectations. Their names went on the paper next to their brilliance. How cool! As my interest peeked viewing this list, she was off to an appointment. She gave me approval to take a picture.

S O C I A L C O N T R A C T S
Brilliant – 7B

Honesty	Effort
Active listening	Be positive
Communication	No putdowns
Trust	Be responsible
Use self control	Use teamwork
Maturely	Compromise
With Care	Respect
Treat fairly	Love all people

As class began, attendance taken and students were able to pronounce my name, I immediately asked them about their SOCIAL CONTRACTS. Boy, did they want to talk. Generally, the same description as their teacher had provided. What was new was their desire to discuss the "brilliant" students and the ones who were not. They were obviously aware of who was "caring" and treating others "fairly" thus meeting their contracts and who were not. I shut down the discussion at that point with positives regarding their work and its importance. Wished I could have taught them a lesson on this subject, but in hindsight being a high school teacher, maybe not a good idea.

Driving home after school thinking about the 7th graders, I assumed our K −12 schools were instilling citizenship, appropriate behavior, and caring attitudes, in one way or the other. I've now witnessed students at all of levels of learning having love for their friends (Philia). Then I wondered, if our schools are committed to teaching this, and students are applying their learning, why do many students stray as adults. For these students, we need to look back at their parenting, a "conversation" our society seems to avoid. It's as if in some cases, we have given up on the parent's responsibility for their children's growth and behavior. Hope I'm wrong, but if so, missed the dialogue.

First Corinthians 13:13 states that love is greater than even faith and hope. Colossians 3:14 says, "But above all these things put on love, which is the bond of perfection. Love does not delight in evil but rejoices with the truth. It always protects, always trusts, always hopes, always perseveres."[97]

---

[97] http//biblegateway.com//internet/1 Corinthians 13−14 (New International Version (NIV)/

Many scripture passages discuss love in great detail, with emphasis on each of us returning to God the love he provides us, as well as loving ourselves and one another.

As human beings, are we capable of this love? If so, the world and everything we know of it can dramatically change. If not, we remain in war, conflict, and division.

And if we believe that love can unify us and is necessary for our survival, how do we affect such change across the globe?

The first three verses of 1 Corinthians 13 describe this: "If I speak in the tongues of men and of angels, but have not love, I am a noisy gong or a clanging cymbal. And if I have prophetic powers, and understand all mysteries and all knowledge, and if I have all faith, so as to remove mountains, but have not love, I am nothing. If I give away all I have, and if I deliver up my body to be burned, but have not love, I gain nothing."[98]

Paul's point is clear: It doesn't matter what we say, do, or have—if we lack love, we have nothing. If we love, we have it all. Love is important to each and every one of us.

From the poem, "Love Binds"

> "No rope or cable on earth can bind as fast as
> a single thread of love. It is too strong for any
> mortal to describe — except in one word: God,
> for "God is Love." It is a golden thread the

---

98 http//biblia.com//internet/1 Corinthians 13:1–13/The Way of Love//

world's most unifying quality, which makes each part of all." –Anonymous

One of my favorite holiday songs is "Grown-Up Christmas List." In the song, an adult addresses Santa Claus, with what the title indicates—an adult list of Christmas wishes. The chorus goes as follows:

No more lives torn apart

That wars would never start

And time would heal all hearts

Every man would have a friend

That right would always win

And love would never end

This is my grown-up Christmas list

CONCLUSION

As far back in history as one can examine, from sea to sea, in the many different cultures, the idea of fairness has been explored, and innumerable people have uttered the oft-repeated words: "It's not fair." Although we learn at an early age that life isn't always fair, we continue to expect and demand fairness and become disappointed when it's denied. Life isn't always fair, and we know it. Even so, we show our emotions and feelings, sleep on it, time passes, and we reawaken to dust ourselves off and begin another day. You may say, "But it's not easy." You're right; often it isn't. Yet what choice do we have? Remember—time itself is a great healer.

Understanding the difference between equality and equity guides us to living a more balanced life, better able to cope with unfairness. Equality in life is a must; equity is a luxury.

Justice determines the administration of fairness. Justice is the umbrella, and fairness is simply the handle we hold onto. The concept of justice differs throughout the nations and cultures of our world, dependent upon how people want to live. In America, our ethics and values determine justice.

In reality, each of us are responsible and accountable for our own perceptions of justice and fairness. Our willingness and ability to learn from our mistakes and from others, think for ourselves, speak up respectfully, and make necessary changes in our lives will aid us in better understanding the concept of justice and its relevance in our lives. We'll always be the country "we the people" choose to be.

Social problems, in one form or another, will always confront us. Due to today's technology and organized social groups, our recognition of social problems is heightened and more intense than ever. This strong awareness of social concerns is likely to grow throughout the world, challenging us daily to try and solve them.

It's important to confront social issues in a positive, collaborative way, and as challenges rather than problems. When doing so, confidence and enthusiasm flourish instead of frustration and despair, and an "us against them" mentality, so often observed. Certain social issues may be solved by changing our own attitudes, if we're willing to consider all other people above ourselves. Current division in our daily lives, red and blue, is preventing our own progress and welfare. Our nation cries for leadership!

Regardless of how people perceive the world around them, we'll all experience suffering, grief, and pain. My intent with this writing isn't to preach religion or manifest your faith. However, if you believe in God, then there's a reason for God in your life. And during your most difficult times, trust God and let him into your life.

I believe that regardless of how many slogans and "experts" describe living a happy and successful life, those with faith and a love for others are the happiest. These people have found balance and contentment in their lives. They've determined their priorities and values, and they're realists, rarely extremists, and able to cope with everyday life's ups and downs.

Serving and caring for others brings happiness to people. We're not born with this quality. We learn to love one another, or we learn to be suspicious and hate. Therefore, each human being has a choice in life.

Furthermore, happy people are more prone to be accepting and tolerant people. They have a purpose in life and a desire each day to keep learning and growing. They see the good in people and have positive relationships. They live with hope and faith rather than fear and daily discomfort. Happy people look forward to tomorrow's challenges.

Believing that we have a purpose and meaning in life strengthens our ability to lead healthy, productive lives. Our faith and trust in God gives us strength, courage, and stability. We all experience changes at different stages in our lives; we know it when it happens. The question is, how do we respond?

Our lives are constantly changing, whether we like it or not. Embracing change with a positive attitude, by overcoming stress and negativity, is the healthiest response. When change challenges you, keep in mind the most important things in your life, check your mental and physical health, look to simplify your life, focus on what you can control, communicate your feelings with others, and appreciate the wonderful things in your life.

There is no one else in the world like you! Me, myself, and I! Find and use your God given skills and abilities, and then use them to serve others.

With faith, we're better able to live without hate, see the good in others, and find the ability in our hearts to forgive. Faith makes us people of action, with the confidence and courage to act on our own beliefs. Think about it: if more people had faith, what a difference it would make worldwide. For the first time our prayers for peace and justice on earth would be answered.

Our hope is intertwined with our faith, though they're different. Hope is logical thought based on facts and a confident expectation and desire for something positive to occur. Faith is a blind resolution that no matter how the facts, the best outcome will always prevail.

When we have faith and hope, we're capable of loving. Love is the most powerful emotion we can experience. Love expresses a human virtue that is based on human compassion, affection, and kindness—it's our state of being. With love, you get out what you put into it.

Don't allow fear due to past mistakes or regrets prevent you from showing others your love. No one has lived a perfect life. People are perceptive and forgiving and see others for who they are today. Every day is a new day to strengthen one's love and be willing and able to share it with others.

Never forget the vast accomplishments of the American people, those men and women, of all races and creeds, who courageously served their country to keep it free, secure, and safe. Never forget that the vast majority of Americans want the same thing today: freedom, equality, and the opportunity for success and the pursuit of happiness. Never forget, when formulating opinions regarding social issues, to be informed, to scrutinize social media and news, and to think for yourself. Ask yourself: am I basing my opinions and actions on what's best for the majority of Americans, or on my political opinions, needs, and wants?

Social issues always have been and will continue to be. But today's social issues can be resolved. The question is, how will Americans deal with these issues? Will we eventually determine who we are as one people "under God, indivisible, with liberty and justice for all." Then, and only then, will our nation be ready to take the next step towards leading and unifying the world in peace and love. America's destiny?